RIVER OF WORDS

MUSINGS ON PORT ROYAL SOUND THROUGH POETRY AND ART

Produced by Students of Beaufort County School District

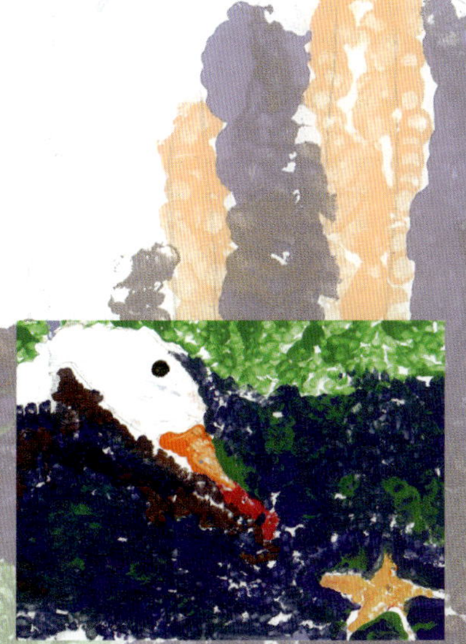

Deahn Holmes
Lady's Island Elementary
3rd Grade

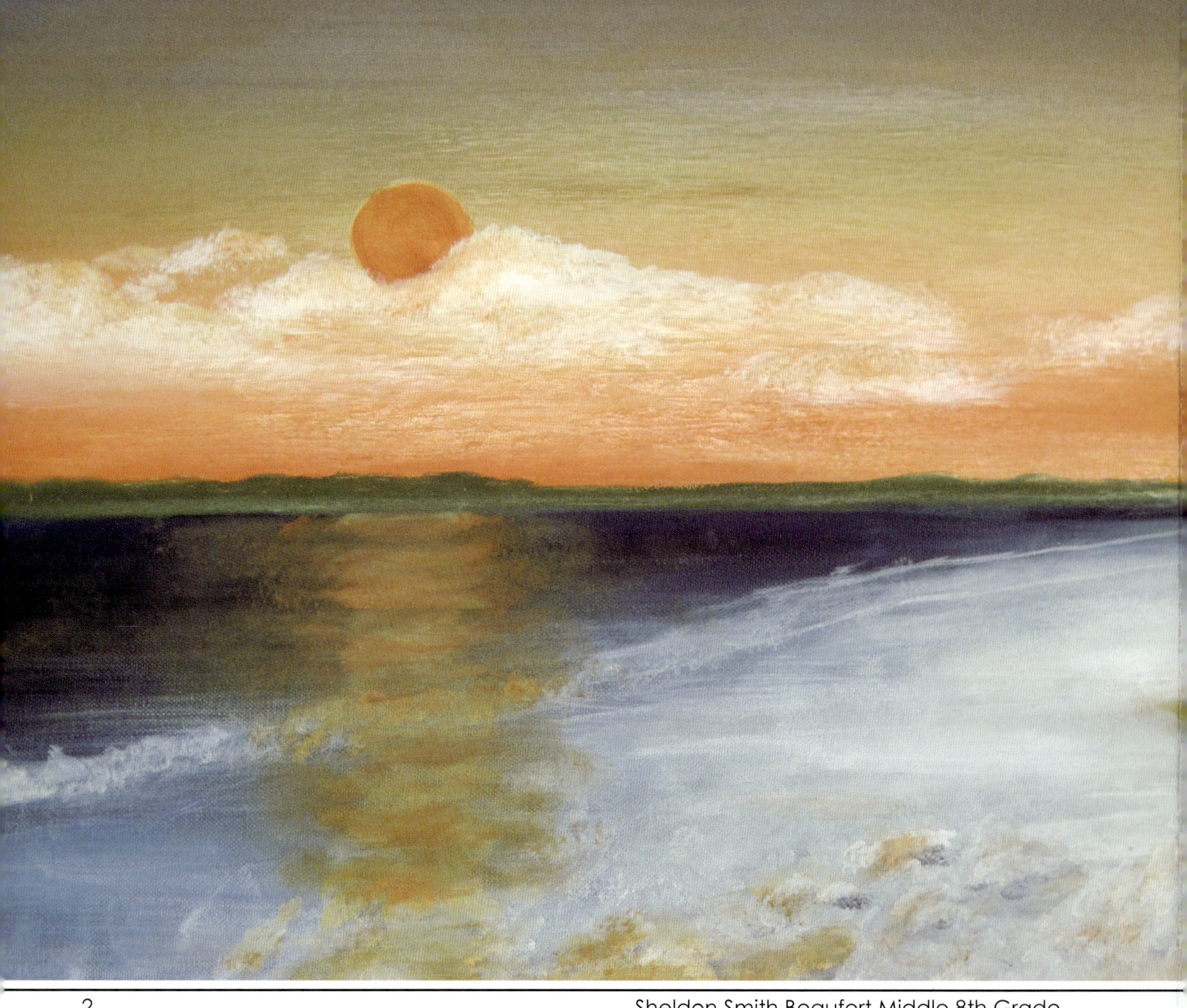

Sheldon Smith Beaufort Middle 8th Grade

Before their minds have been marinated in the culture of television, consumerism, shopping malls, computers and freeways, children can find magic in trees, water, animals, landscapes and their own places.

David W. Orr, Chair of Environmental Studies, Oberlin College

River of Words: Musings on Port Royal Sound Through Poetry and Art is a tangible demonstration of true community engagement in the learning process. Students from kindergarten through high school from all corners of Beaufort County had the privilege of studying alongside naturalists, scientists, artists, authors, and fishermen. These talented volunteers contributed to our children's grasp of the uniqueness of the Port Royal Sound ecosystem. We are proud that this imaginative, intergenerational effort engaged so many of Beaufort County's finest.

Numerous enduring understandings resulted from this multidisciplinary study. An understanding of the interdependency of people with nature in the Lowcountry is underscored in students' writings and artwork. An appreciation of the delicate balance needed to protect and nurture the environment was built through students' active engagement. A commitment to sustainability of the natural environment was evident in children's experiences.

While this book is a culminating tribute to the students and their work, the true outcome of their learning will be realized over the years as they grow, apply their knowledge, and advocate for this special place we call home.

Valerie Truesdale, Ph. D.
Superintendent

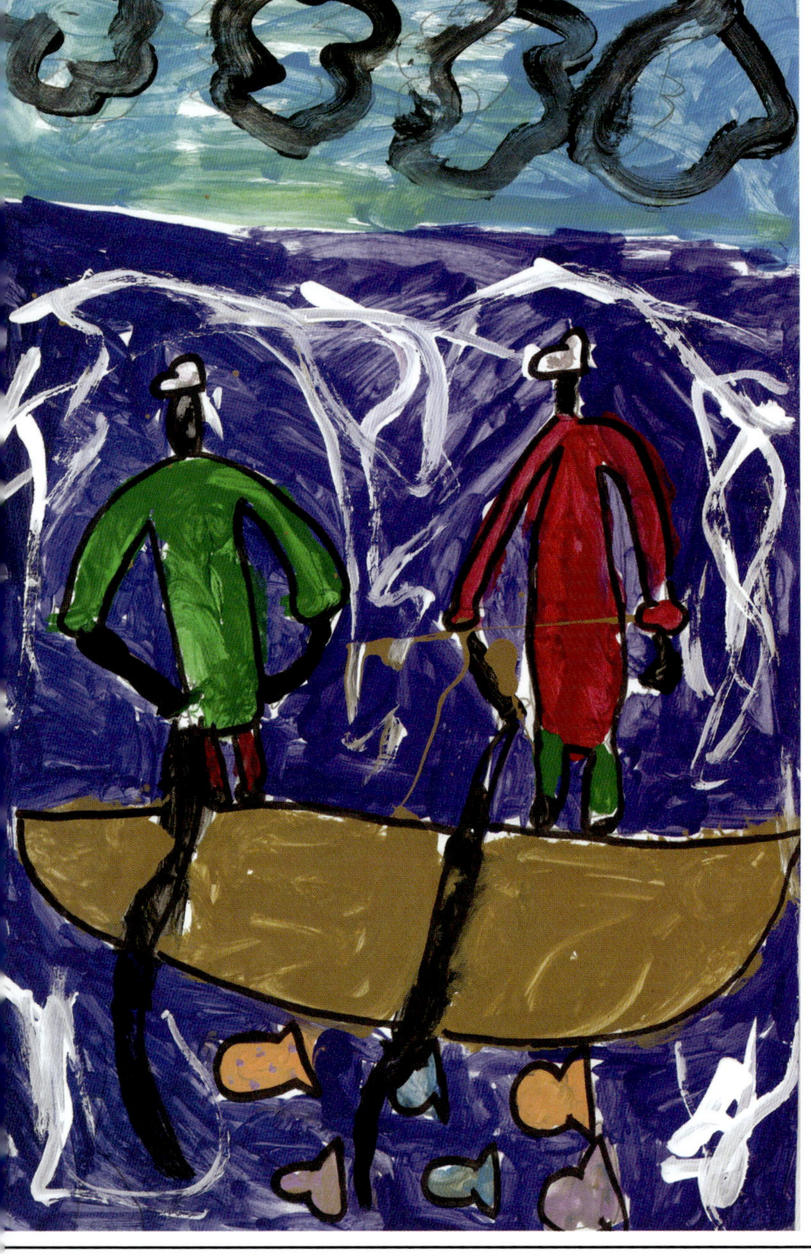

Who we are as a nation, region and community is largely defined by the local landscape and culture. This complex relationship between people and place shapes each of us. It affects who we are and how we live our lives. It influences our imaginations and the kind of art, music and literature we create. Because so much of our identity is tied to place, it is important that our Lowcountry youth are knowledgeable about the uniqueness of the Port Royal Sound as they develop their own "sense of place." To this end, 130 teachers from fifteen Beaufort County schools designed a place-based, experiential curriculum, ultimately engaging 2,400 Kindergarten through twelfth grade students in Science, Social Studies, Math, Language and Visual Art explorations and interpretations of the environment.

Colton Kent Hilton Head Island Elementary 3rd Grade

Beaufort County's once-agrarian society has given way to the conveniences of the 21st century; consequently, our children spend a great deal of time indoors and online. Their "sense of place" is at risk of becoming a lost part of their identity. However, thanks to the generous support of master naturalists who provided teacher workshops, guided field studies, and donated resources, students learned first-hand about the ecology of their own school campuses and neighborhoods.

Following the guidelines of the national **River of Words** program, schools from across the county volunteered to pilot the program. Each crafted a unique approach to teaching and learning about nearby ecosystems. With Science at the heart of learning, creativity boomed! Students explored the salt marsh and maritime forests, researched the interdependency of ecosystems, mapped local waterways, tested salinity levels, measured tidal amplitudes, journaled outdoor observations, interviewed shrimpers, compared the Port Royal Sound to other coastal watersheds, and debated the inevitable clash of economic and ecological forces.

After observing, probing, researching, recording and directly experiencing their natural environment, students returned to classrooms to demonstrate their newfound "sense of place" through art and creative writing. Beaufort County School District's **River of Words 2010-2011** project launched in September to celebrate National Literacy Month and culminated in the spring with student exhibitions of original poems and artwork during Youth Art and National Poetry Months.

As with the student exhibitions, ***River of Words: Musings on Port Royal Sound Through Poetry And Art*** is a testament to the power of an integrated curriculum that makes learning relevant and enables students to create and internalize their own knowledge. It demonstrates the added value of collaborating with community resources. And above all, it shows appreciation of this very special "ecological address" from the children who live there.

Enjoy!

BROWN SHRIMP

I am tired
Always running
My travels are limited
Trying to stay alive
Living on plankton and pluff mud
I am prey to everything around me
If I sleep I might not wake
I see everything around me
I am very cautious of every move I make

Chase Phillips
H.E. McCracken Middle
8th Grade

CORE BEAUTY

Against the current
Only his eyes remain above the surface
Even strokes and
Strong kicks
Guide him upstream
As he swims with slow and easy motions
Only the core beauty shows
Then, everything irrelevant
Drifts away
Through the water

Jackilynn Ritchie
Beaufort Middle
8th Grade

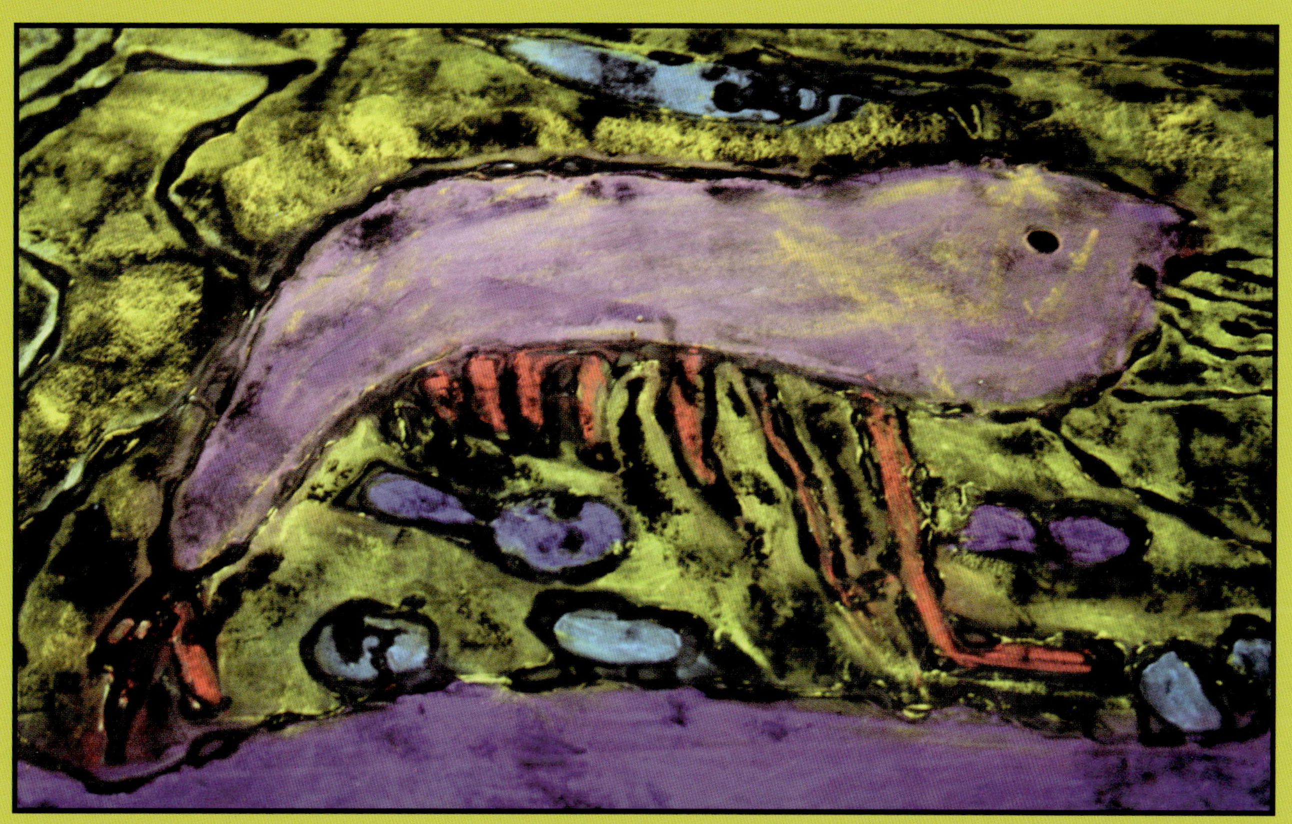

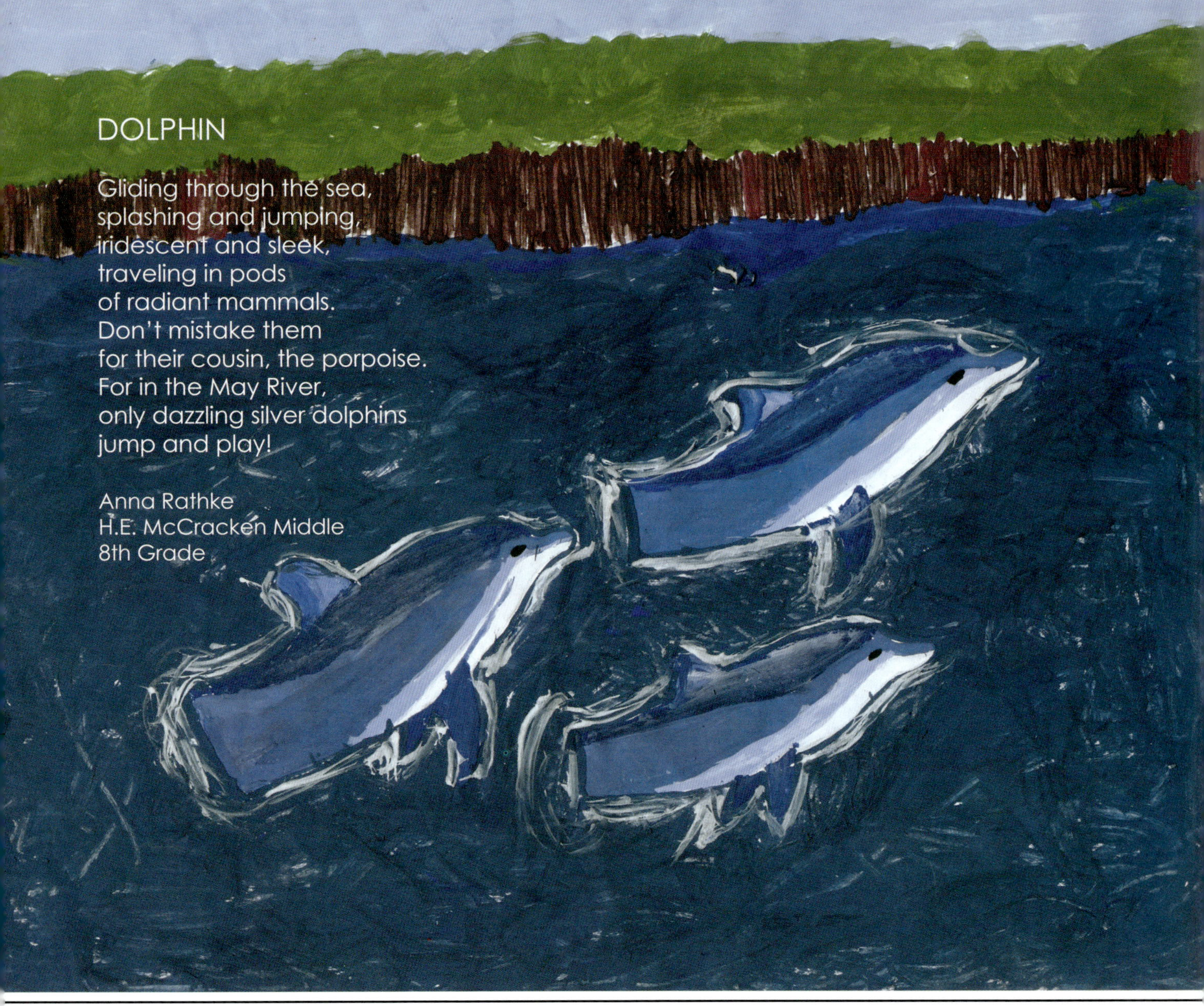

Karla Hernandez Bluffton Middle 7th Grade

ENJOYMENT

Many jellyfish,
Just having fun.
Trying to get back
To their homes,
Gently moving
With the water.

The teacher trying
To catch crabs
While amusing us.
Crabs too smart
To go into the traps.

Loon fishing for a bite
Looking beautiful as ever,
Having a great time
Showing off.

Kids enjoying the day
Like it is Christmas morning!
Laughing and playing
With their friends.

Reginald Brown
Pritchardville Elementary
5th Grade

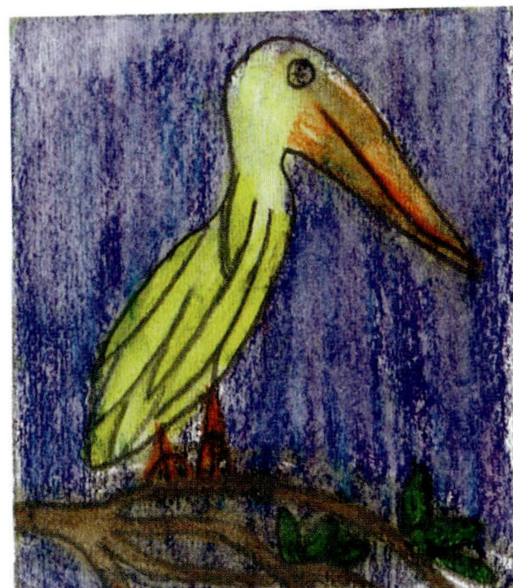

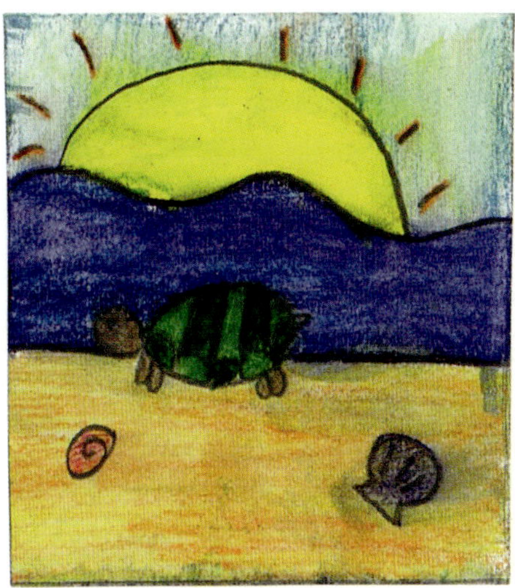

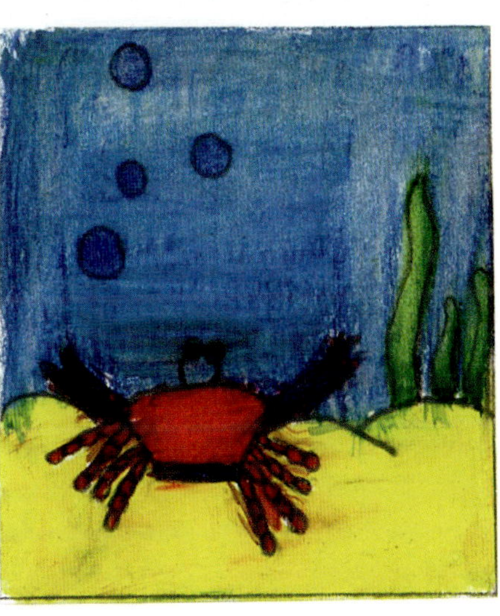

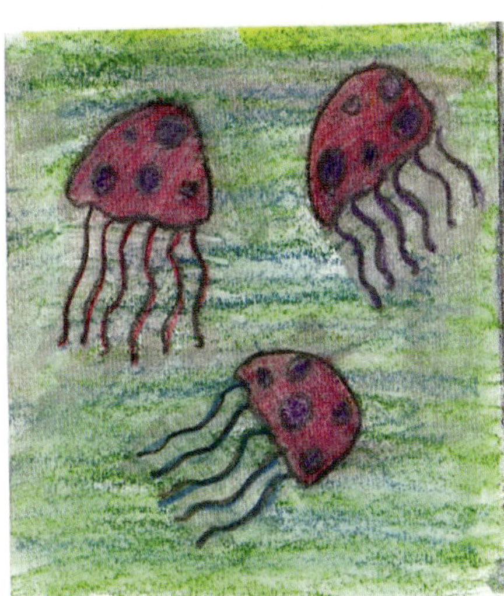

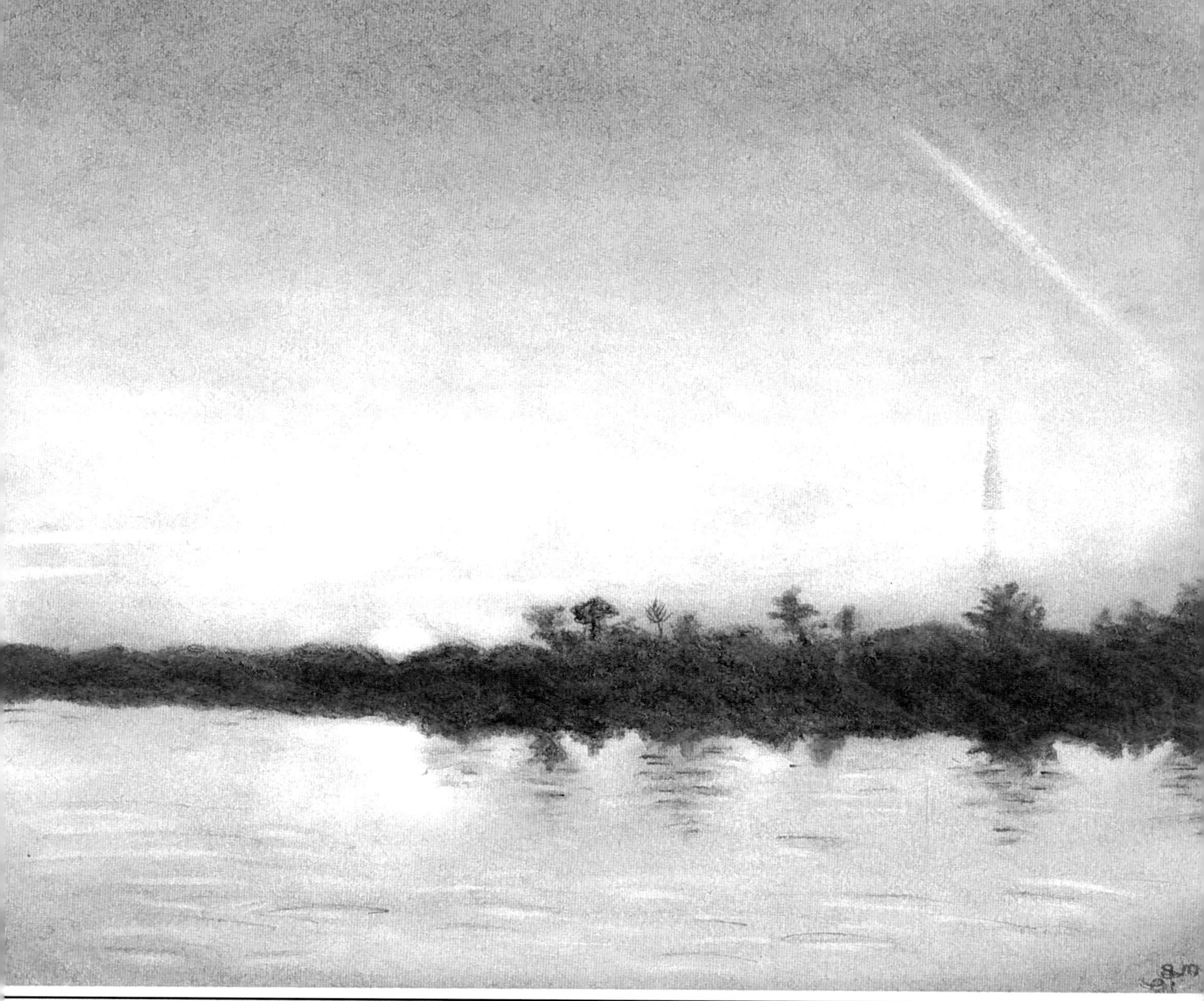

Monica Bowman Beaufort High 12th Grade

WATER WONDERLAND

The rising sun grins brightly upon the sparkling blue waters
As the waves lap and climb up the sides of the kayak;
The marsh grass swaying in the chilling breeze.
A single fish leaps from the water,
Only to splash back down into the depths of its home.
A lone island sits still on its throne surrounded by the river,
Looking lonely yet as magnificent as a king.
In the distance, the gulls laugh as they perch atop the palm,
Flapping their wings and hopping as they frolic and play.
The sun blazes, laughing with the birds and stopping the cold breeze;
The warmth making everything more alive.
The waves and ripples still and cease,
Letting the sparkles shine bright,
Giving it the look of a Wonderland.

Ashley Hunt
Beaufort High

A RIVER

You never
Know where
It will go. It's
Wild. It's so
Majestic and
Powerful, but
So helpless
And innocent.
Home to animals
Big and small.
Flows calmly and
Brings joy one
Day, but could be
Merciless and bring
Destruction in a
Second. A River.
Running happily with
Nature.

Morgan Rizer
Bluffton Middle
7th Grade

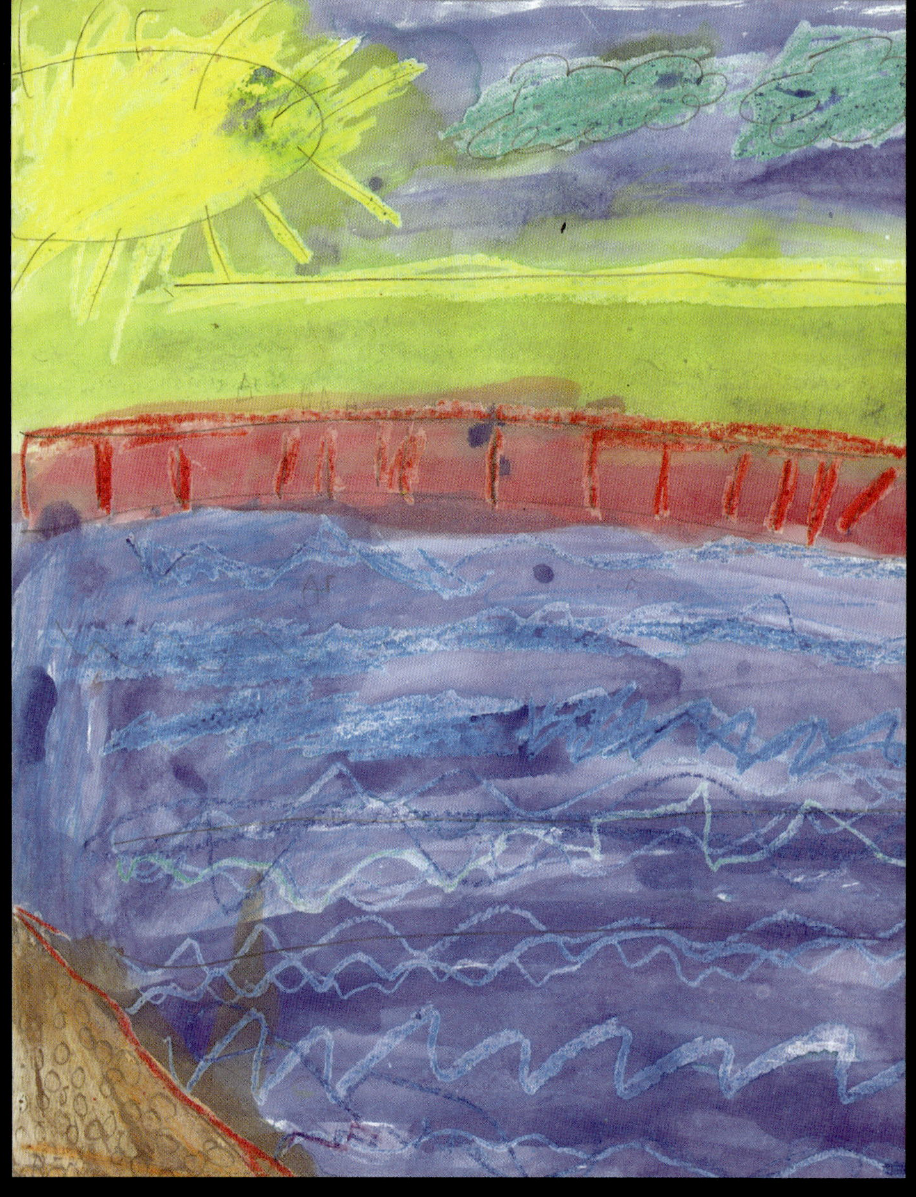

Anaunda Fripp Broad River Elementary 3rd Grade

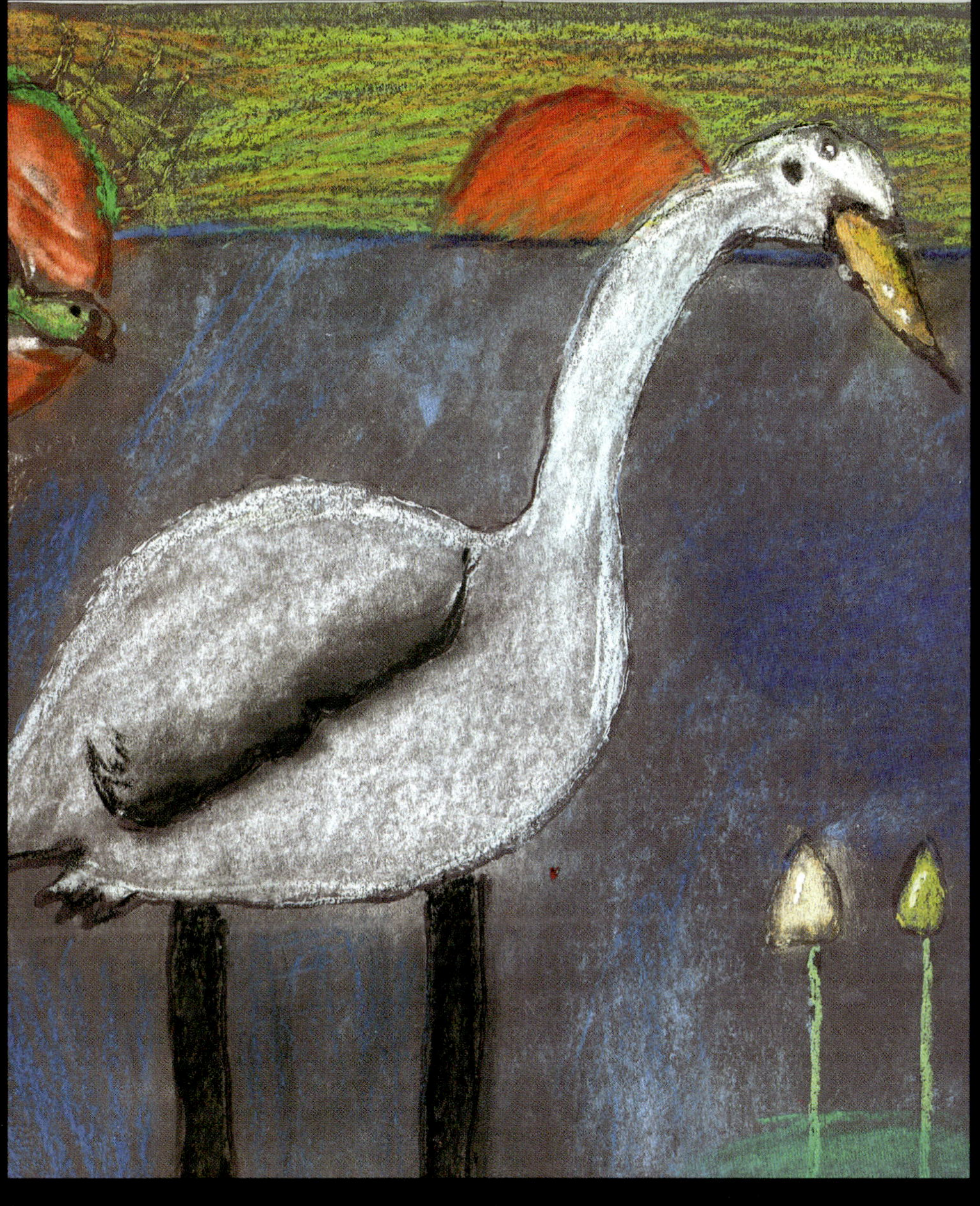

A BEAUTIFUL DAY

Blue herons flying
gracefully
Across the dark, cloudy sky.

Jellyfish swimming
Across the creek
Bumping into one another.

Brown pelicans chilling
Near the marsh
While others
Fly in the sky.

Police sirens
Disturbing the silence
Of the beautiful creek.

Jose Estrada
Pritchardville Elementary
5th Grade

Kenyah Blake Joseph S. Shanklin Elementary 5th Grade

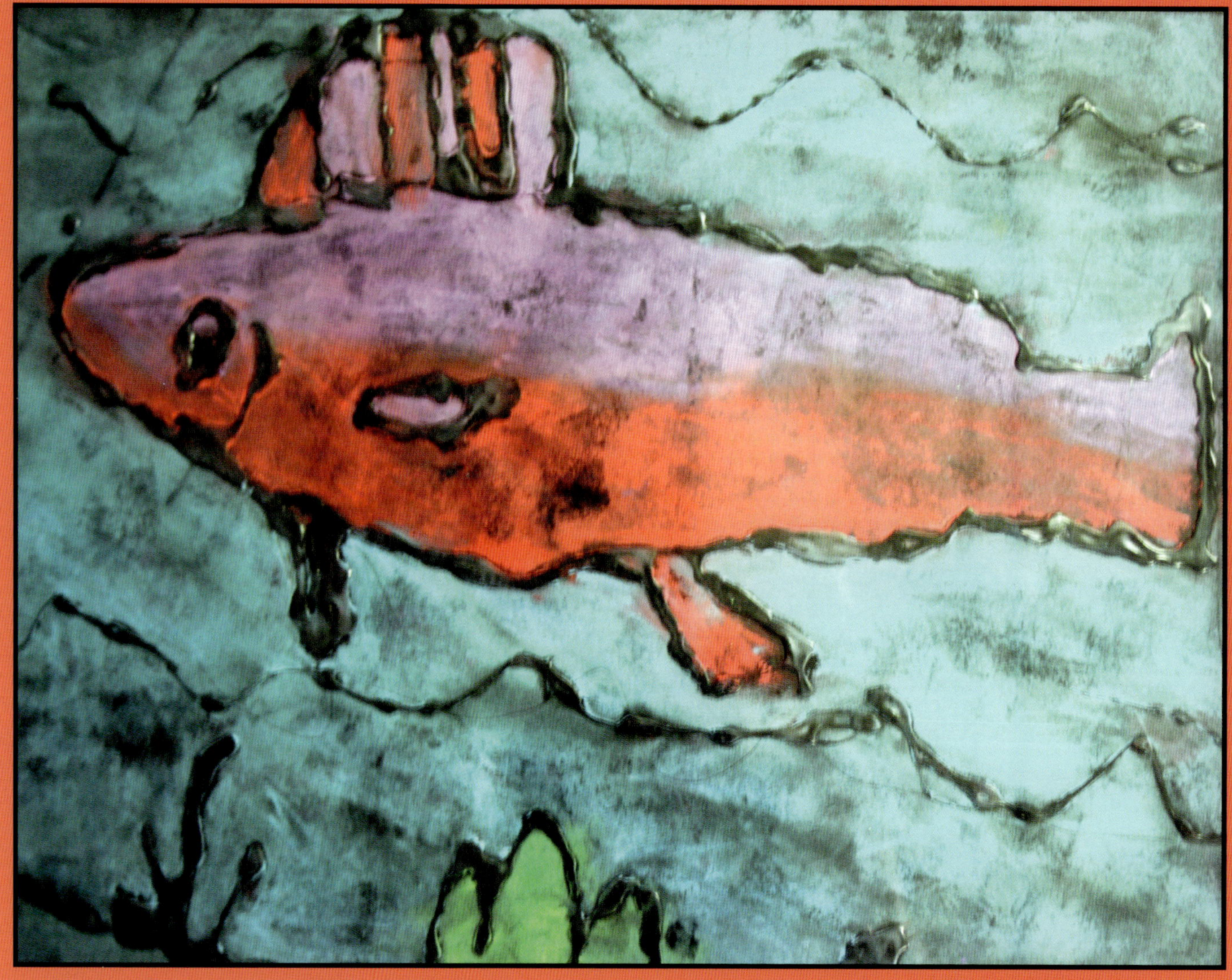

FLOUNDER

Moving its eye from the bottom to the top of its head
Living at the bottom
Always cleaning up messes
Waiting silently as it stalks its prey
Never moving unless necessary
Always hoping that predators don't see it
Living in isolation
For its whole life
Fighting for survival in the ocean
Called LIFE

Angel Lopez
H.E. McCracken Middle
8th Grade

LIFE OF A SEA TURTLE

Starts off as an egg,
Unsure of the dangers above.
From the day it rises from the ground
It's not aware of the predators flying
above.
It drags itself across the beach and
into the ocean.
So life begins for a sea turtle.
Living on its own.
Living up to 100 years.
Laying its own eggs.
A sea turtle.

Andrew Eldridge
Bluffton Middle School
7th Grade

IF I WERE A SEA TURTLE

If I were a sea turtle, I would be 6 centimeters long.

I would hide in the sea with my sea friends.

I would play outside in the river.

I would eat shrimp (13 cm) for breakfast, and use
sand for a blanket.

I would be afraid of dangerous sharks (300 cm).

The most fun thing I would do is play with fish (8 cm)
and little sea turtles (6 cm).

Banessa Lucero (148 cm)
Beaufort Elementary
4th Grade

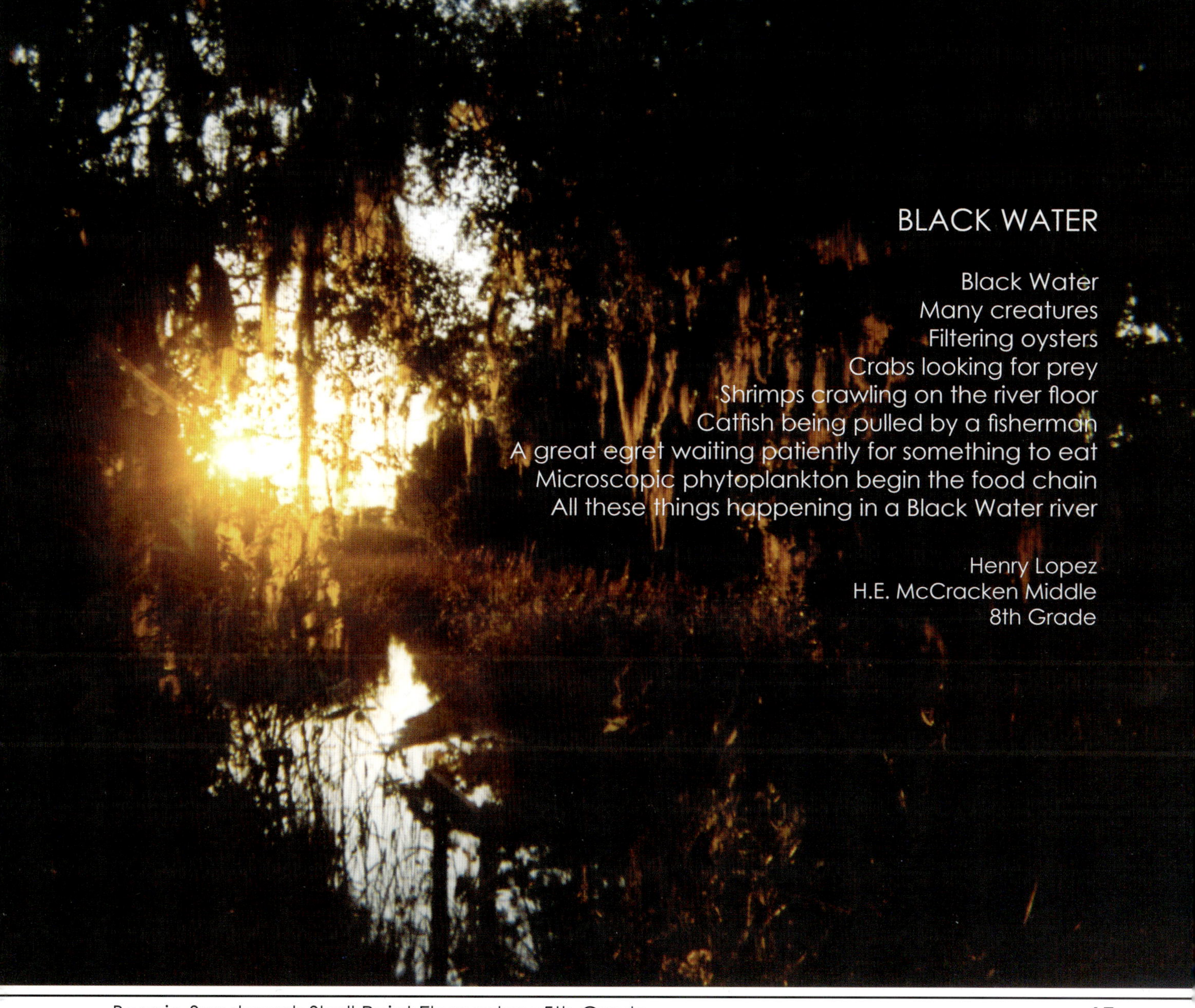

BLACK WATER

Black Water
Many creatures
Filtering oysters
Crabs looking for prey
Shrimps crawling on the river floor
Catfish being pulled by a fisherman
A great egret waiting patiently for something to eat
Microscopic phytoplankton begin the food chain
All these things happening in a Black Water river

Henry Lopez
H.E. McCracken Middle
8th Grade

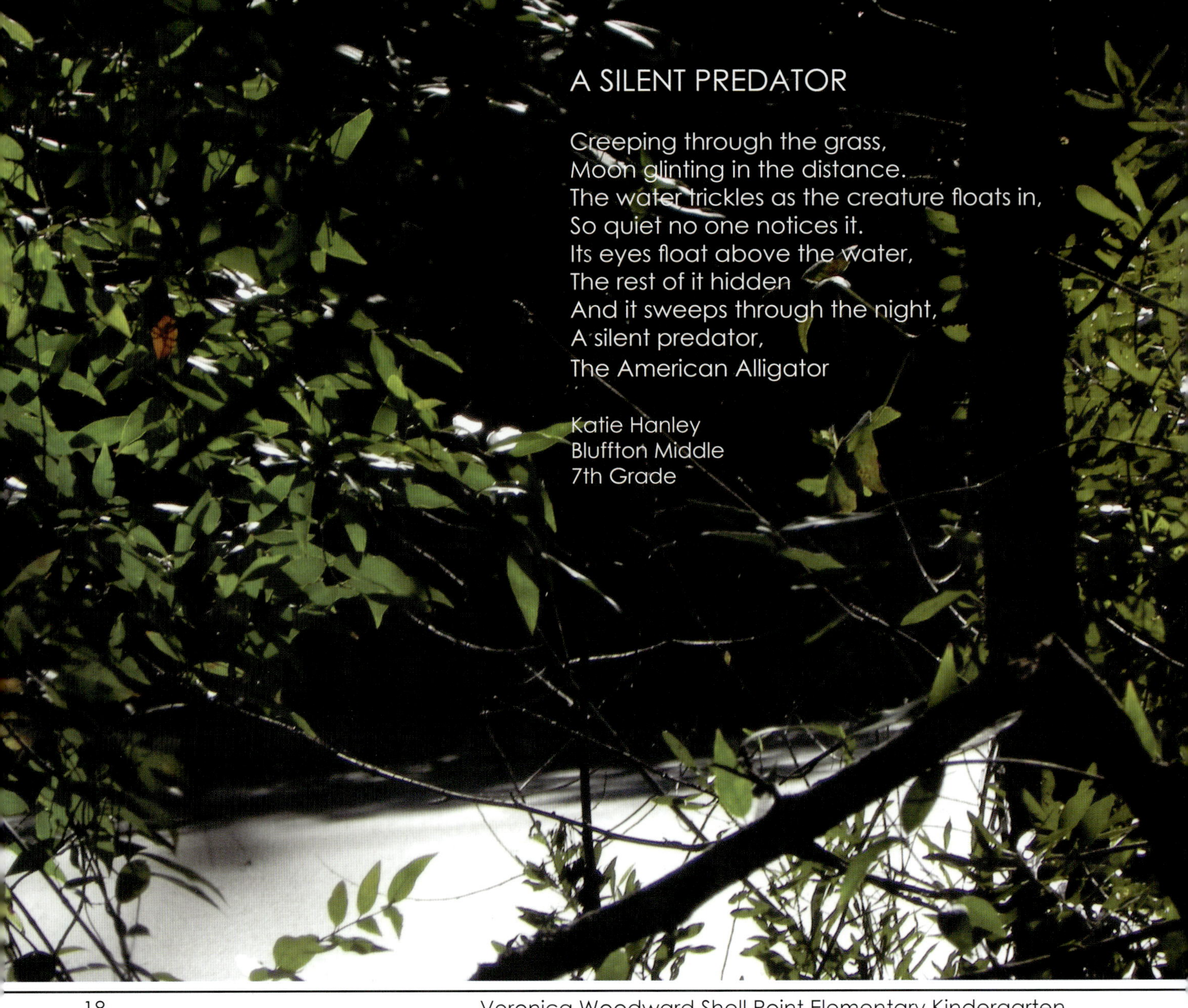

Veronica Woodward Shell Point Elementary Kindergarten

NATURE

The tall grass and trees
Sway in the wind.
The marsh is boggy
With water and mud.
Pelicans perch on branches.
Royal terns flick over rocks
for food at the shore.
Shells and crabs scurry around
As gulls grab fish from the sea.

Ezhri Greggs
Pritchardville Elementary
4th Grade

NATURE'S WAY OF TELLING US

Startled birds flying by
While kids look curiously into the sky.

Wind flowing back and forth,
Can't decide which way to go.

Kids bundling together, freezing,
Trying to watch the water flow.

Birds hiding, kids hiding, trying to stay away
From the cold that is coming today.

Andrew Perez
Pritchardville Elementary
5th Grade

CAMP SEWEE

Snail, snail, what do you see?
I see a ghost crab staring at me.
Ghost crab, ghost crab, what do you see?
I see a raccoon chasing me.
Raccoon, raccoon, what do you see?
I see sand all around me.
Sand, sand what do you see?
I see people stepping on me.
Shells, shells, what do you see?
I see people collecting me.
Sand dunes, sand dunes, what do you see?
I see turtle eggs burying me.
Sweetgrass, sweetgrass what do you see?
I see people making baskets out of me.

Allona Carter
Joseph S. Shanklin Elementary
4th Grade

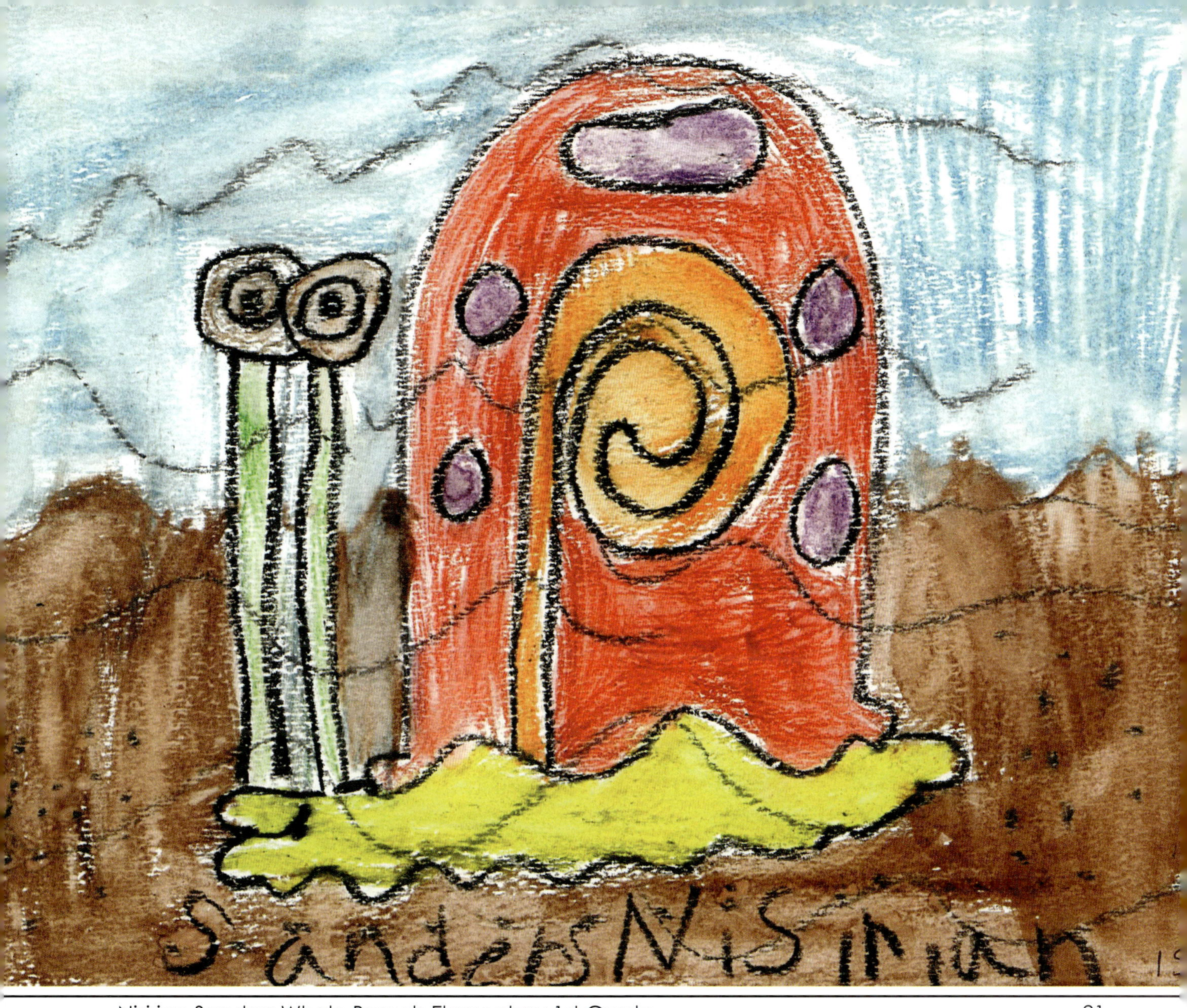

Nisirian Sanders Whale Branch Elementary 1st Grade

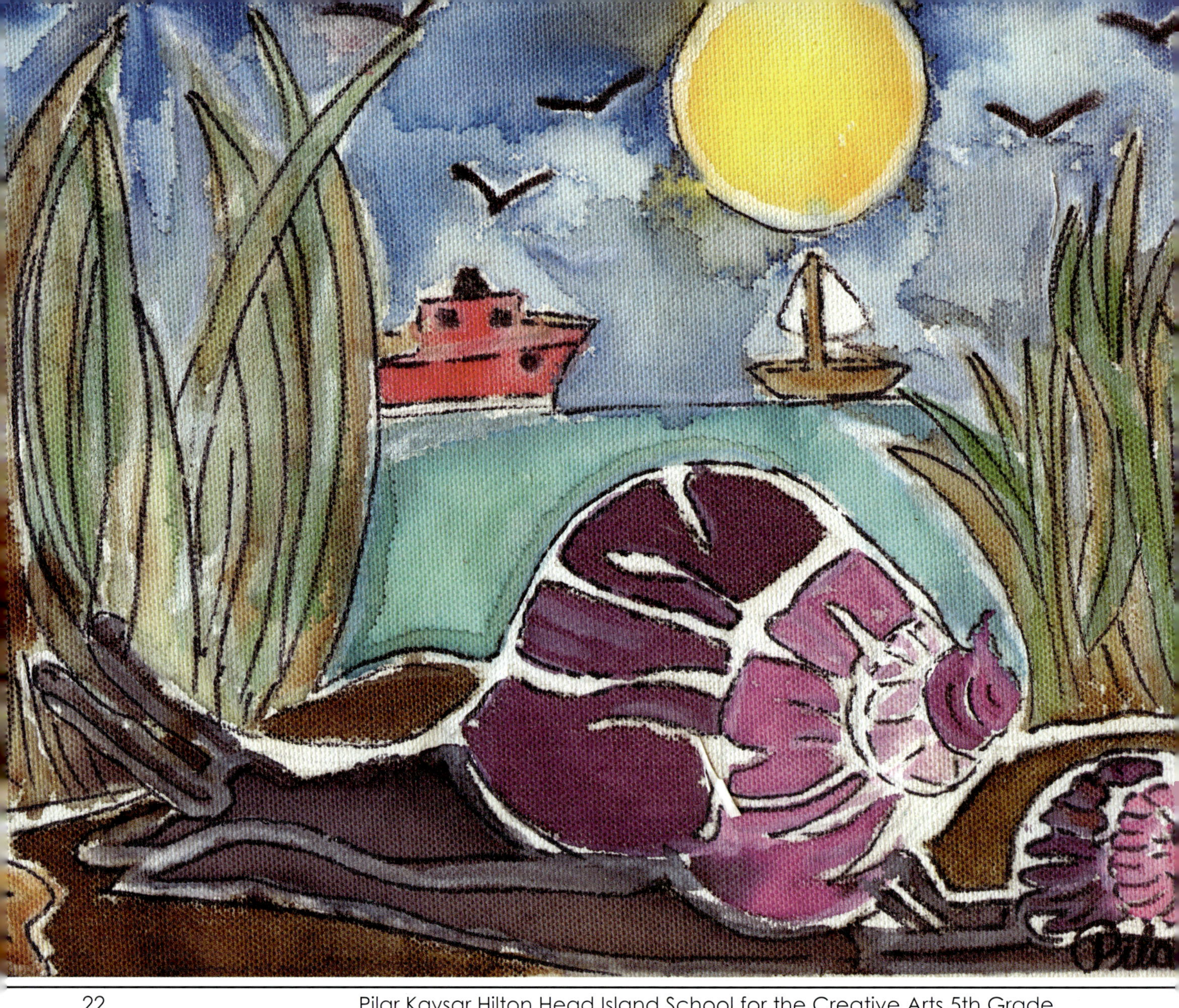

Pilar Kaysar Hilton Head Island School for the Creative Arts 5th Grade

FEELINGS AROUND ME

I am sitting at the shore.
Beneath my toes water slowly comes up but doesn't stay long.
Birds circle over me. Palm trees sway.
Sunshine stings my eyes like a nighttime campfire.
Boats head toward the horizon spraying water
As fish jump trying to escape.
Blue covers the scene.
Waves knock surfers down.
Children laugh as they build forts.
"CAW, CAW, CAW!" birds call from overhead.
On the right of me a big umbrella falls down in the wind.
Whoosh, whoosh!
Waves knock sand castles down.
A little crab goes by pinching his enemy. Pleased, he goes back into the water.
I stand up while my mom pulls my brother away from his enjoyment.
On my left, Dad is struggling with the umbrella.
The beach is saying goodbye.
I laugh as I remember these things,
Protecting my memories of a day at the beach.

Caitlyn Owen
Hilton Head Island Elementary
3rd Grade

GOLDEN PALM TREE

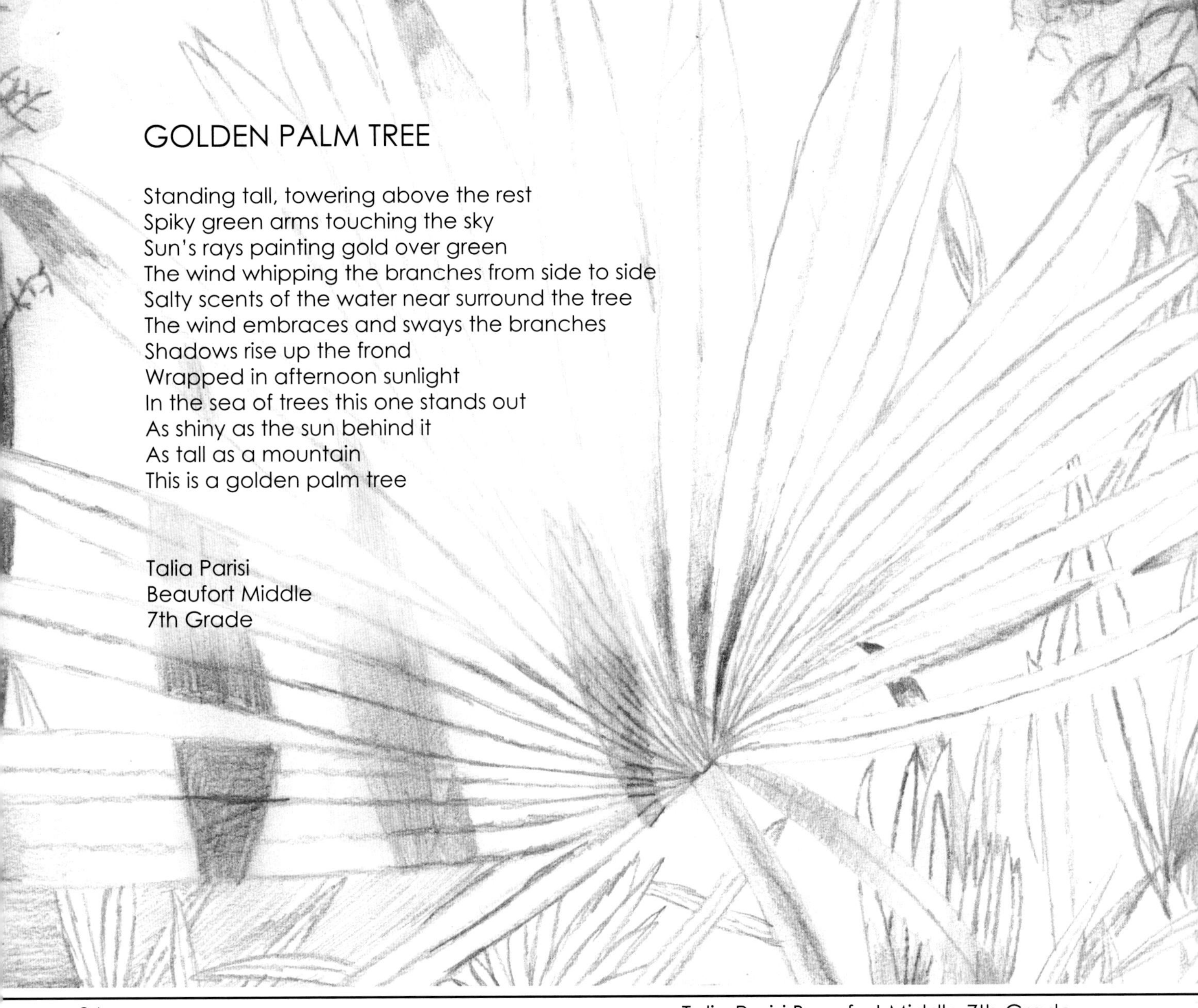

Standing tall, towering above the rest
Spiky green arms touching the sky
Sun's rays painting gold over green
The wind whipping the branches from side to side
Salty scents of the water near surround the tree
The wind embraces and sways the branches
Shadows rise up the frond
Wrapped in afternoon sunlight
In the sea of trees this one stands out
As shiny as the sun behind it
As tall as a mountain
This is a golden palm tree

Talia Parisi
Beaufort Middle
7th Grade

GNARLED BARK

A gloomy crevice between two plates of light
Flaked like crispy burnt waffles.
Layered and dredged, crooked and sharp
Looking lonely and unloved
Sitting quietly on a tree

Guarding its body from fire and frost
Still, sturdy standing strong
Cracked like a dried lake bed

Strong, sweet, and scented
Blunted and blank
Blissfully completing its job

Alex Angus
Beaufort Middle
7th Grade

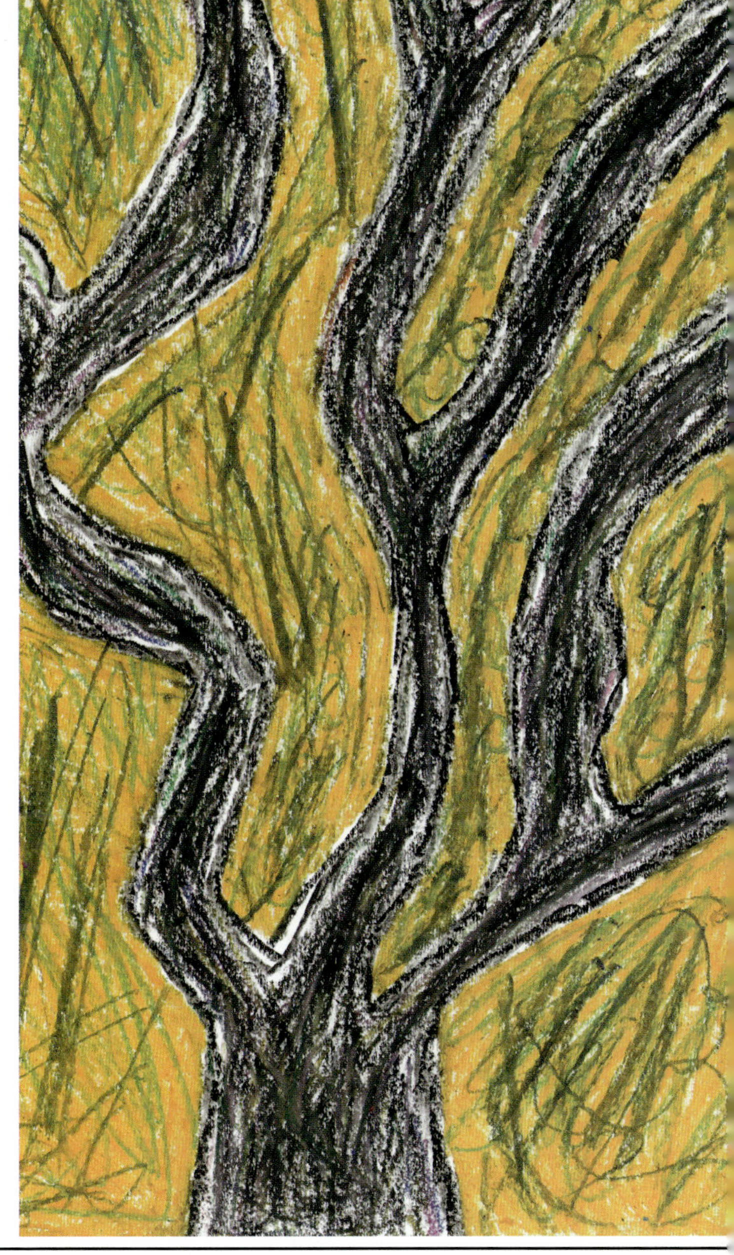

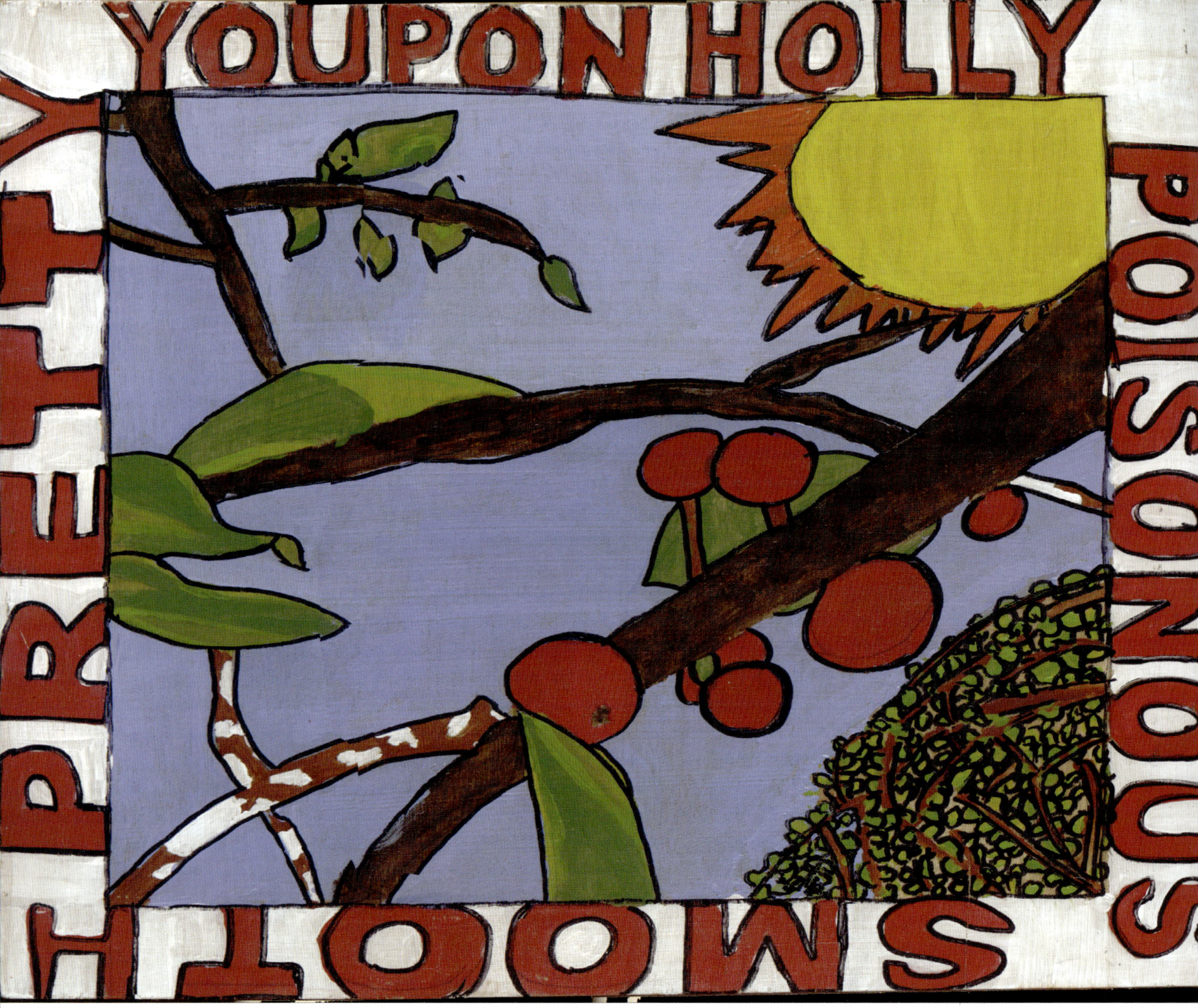

Rachael Reeves Lady's Island Middle 7th Grade

JEWELED PAIN

Your gentle holly leaves rustle with the pine.
An unknown bundle of endless green, with
Your berries red as opened veins.
Your stems appear as thin wisps of twine,
But any animal of your silent forest would know,
You're strong as iron in the hands of man.

The poison jewels held tight to your branch,
Whisper silent voices to beckon invisible hands.
Any forever fears of your forest foes,
Will no longer fulfill forgetful memories.
You cry out to the sky of the deepest blue.
Crash! The calling seas move gently closer.

Speckled in light, rolled in sunshine,
You're company to any unexpected visitor.
You're a flash of poison as if to recall,
A tribe of stout natives devouring your maroon spheres,
As to prove their perfection of strength.
You, my friend, are a symbol of the great, and the corrupt.

Kiara Craner
Beaufort Middle
7th Grade

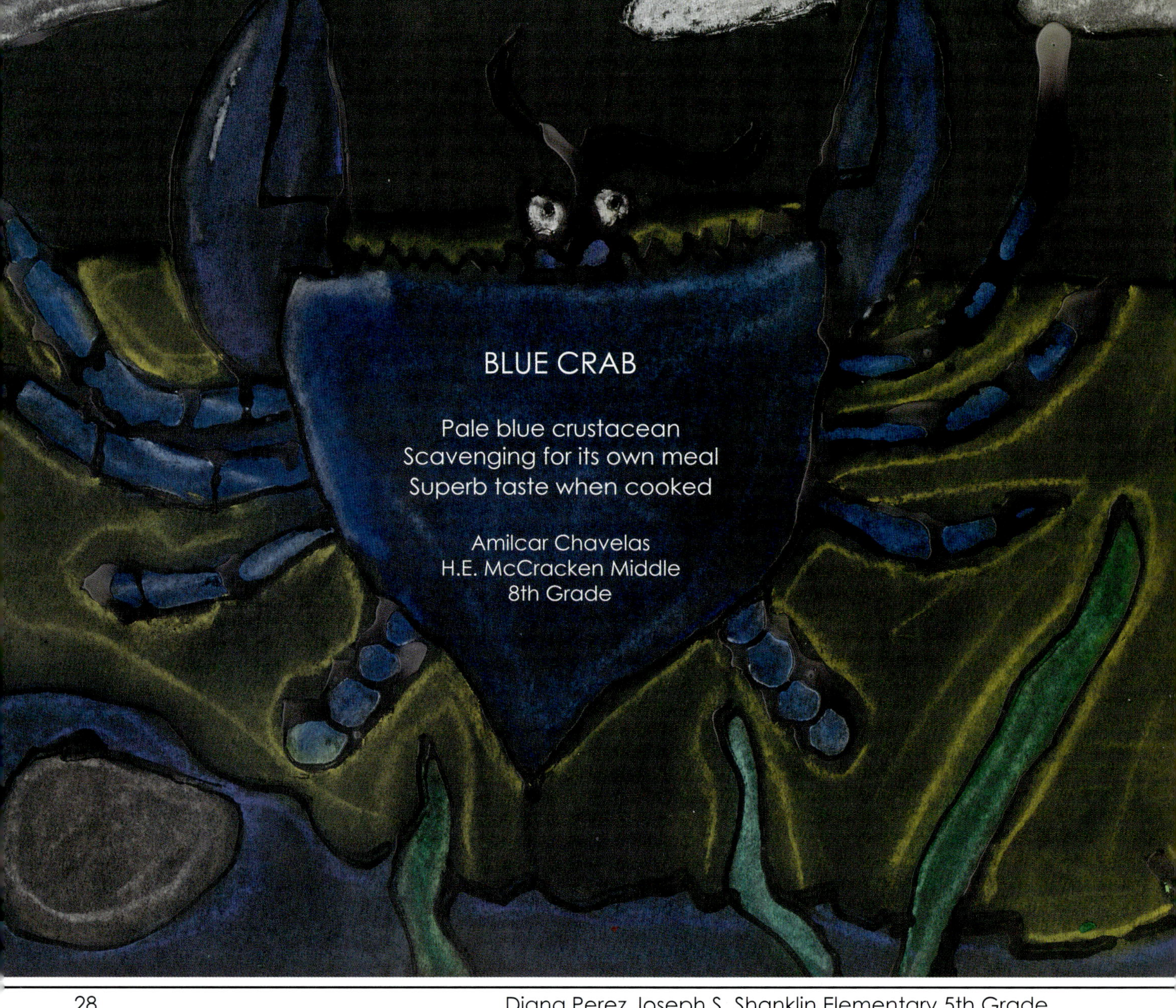

Diana Perez Joseph S. Shanklin Elementary 5th Grade

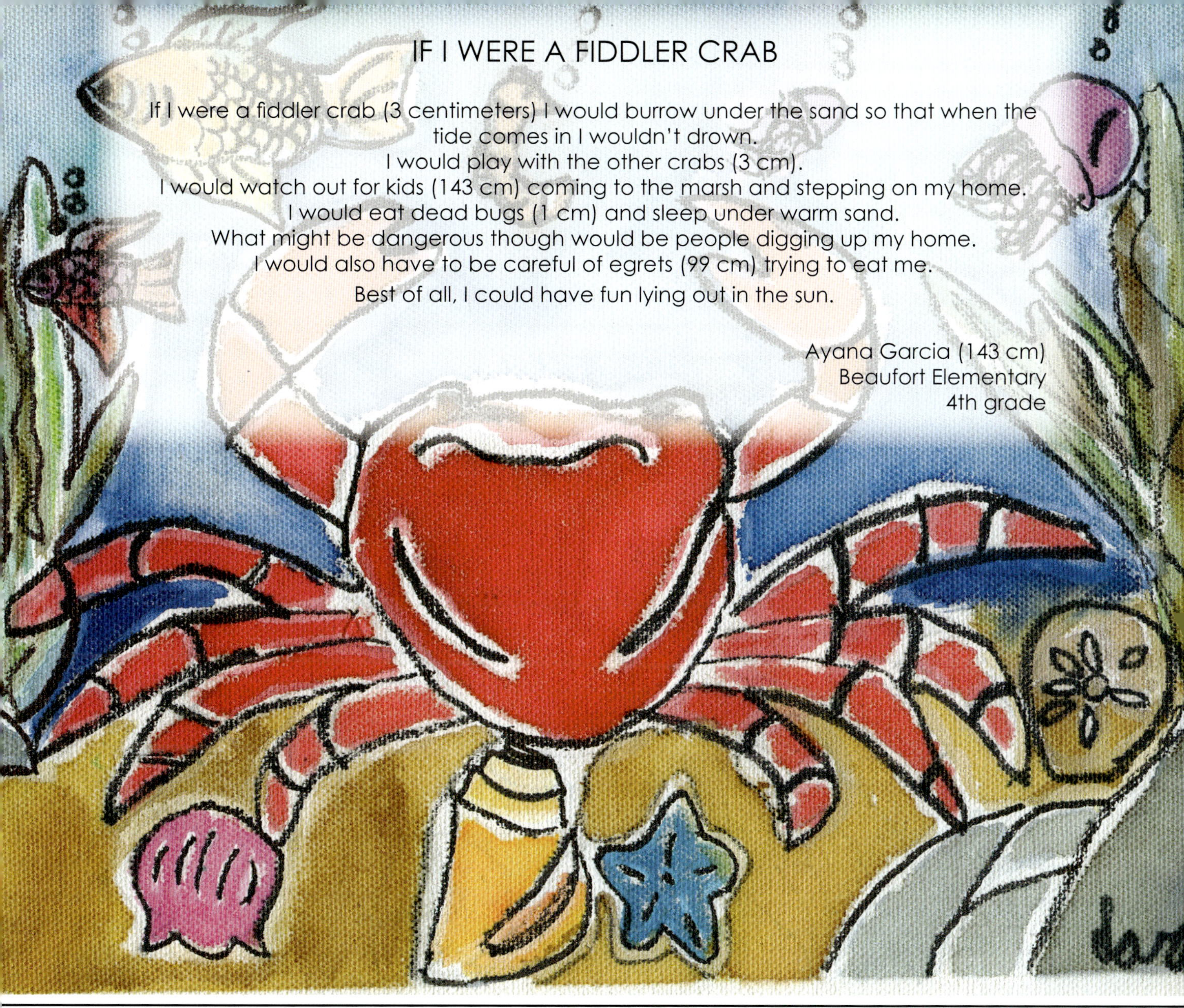

IF I WERE A FIDDLER CRAB

If I were a fiddler crab (3 centimeters) I would burrow under the sand so that when the
tide comes in I wouldn't drown.
I would play with the other crabs (3 cm).
I would watch out for kids (143 cm) coming to the marsh and stepping on my home.
I would eat dead bugs (1 cm) and sleep under warm sand.
What might be dangerous though would be people digging up my home.
I would also have to be careful of egrets (99 cm) trying to eat me.
Best of all, I could have fun lying out in the sun.

Ayana Garcia (143 cm)
Beaufort Elementary
4th grade

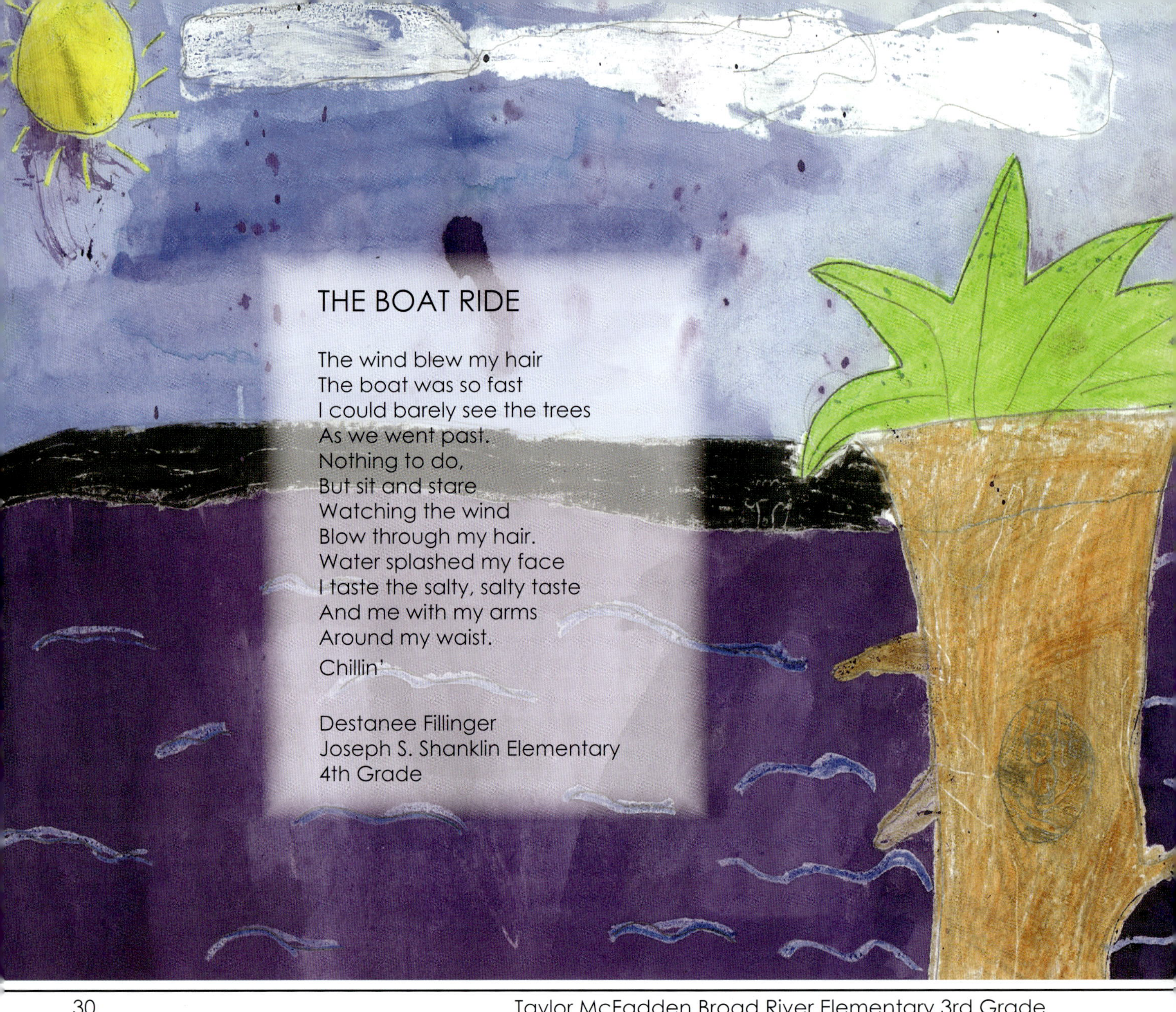

THE BOAT RIDE

The wind blew my hair
The boat was so fast
I could barely see the trees
As we went past.
Nothing to do,
But sit and stare
Watching the wind
Blow through my hair.
Water splashed my face
I taste the salty, salty taste
And me with my arms
Around my waist.
Chillin'

Destanee Fillinger
Joseph S. Shanklin Elementary
4th Grade

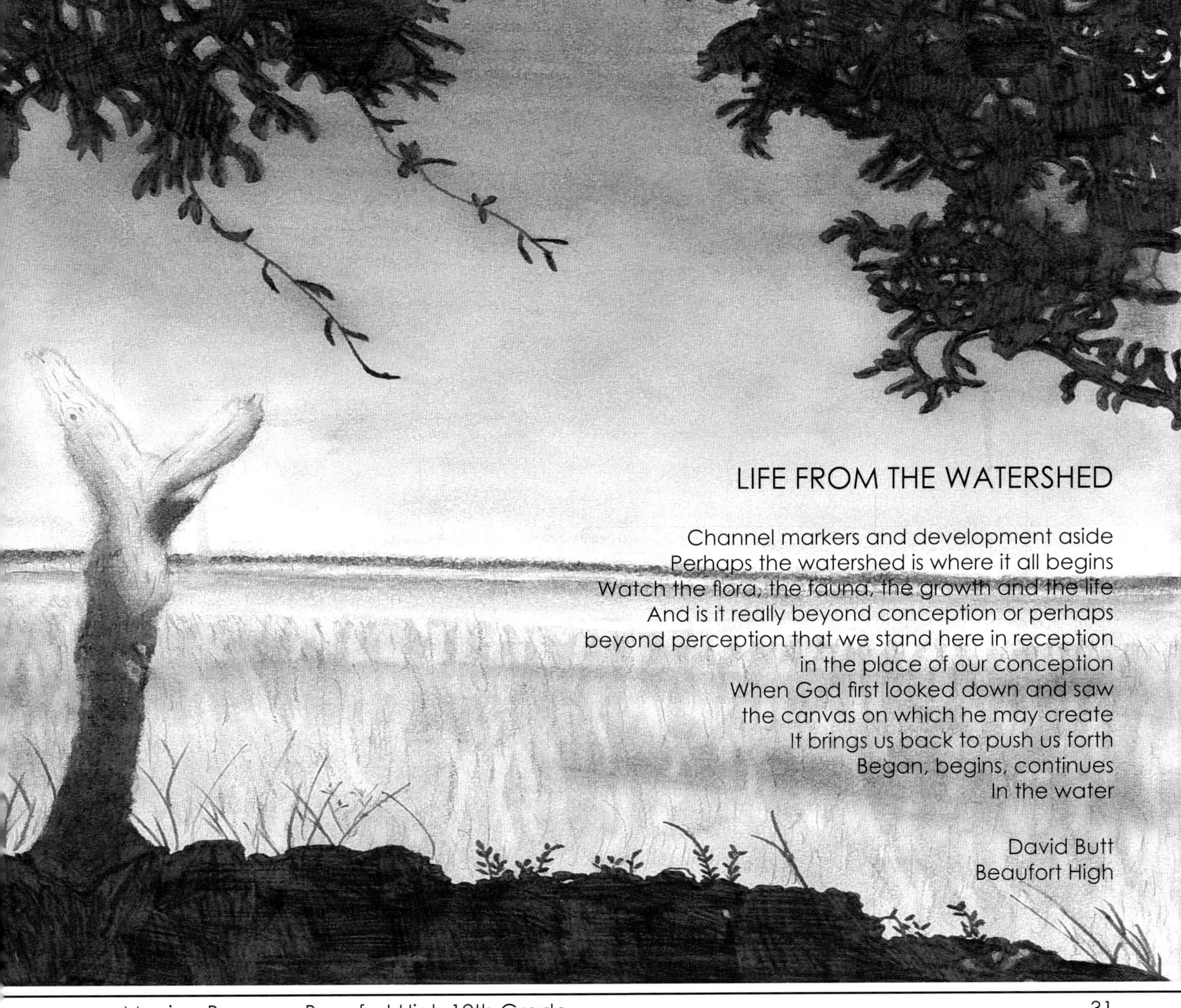

LIFE FROM THE WATERSHED

Channel markers and development aside
Perhaps the watershed is where it all begins
Watch the flora, the fauna, the growth and the life
And is it really beyond conception or perhaps
beyond perception that we stand here in reception
in the place of our conception
When God first looked down and saw
the canvas on which he may create
It brings us back to push us forth
Began, begins, continues
In the water

David Butt
Beaufort High

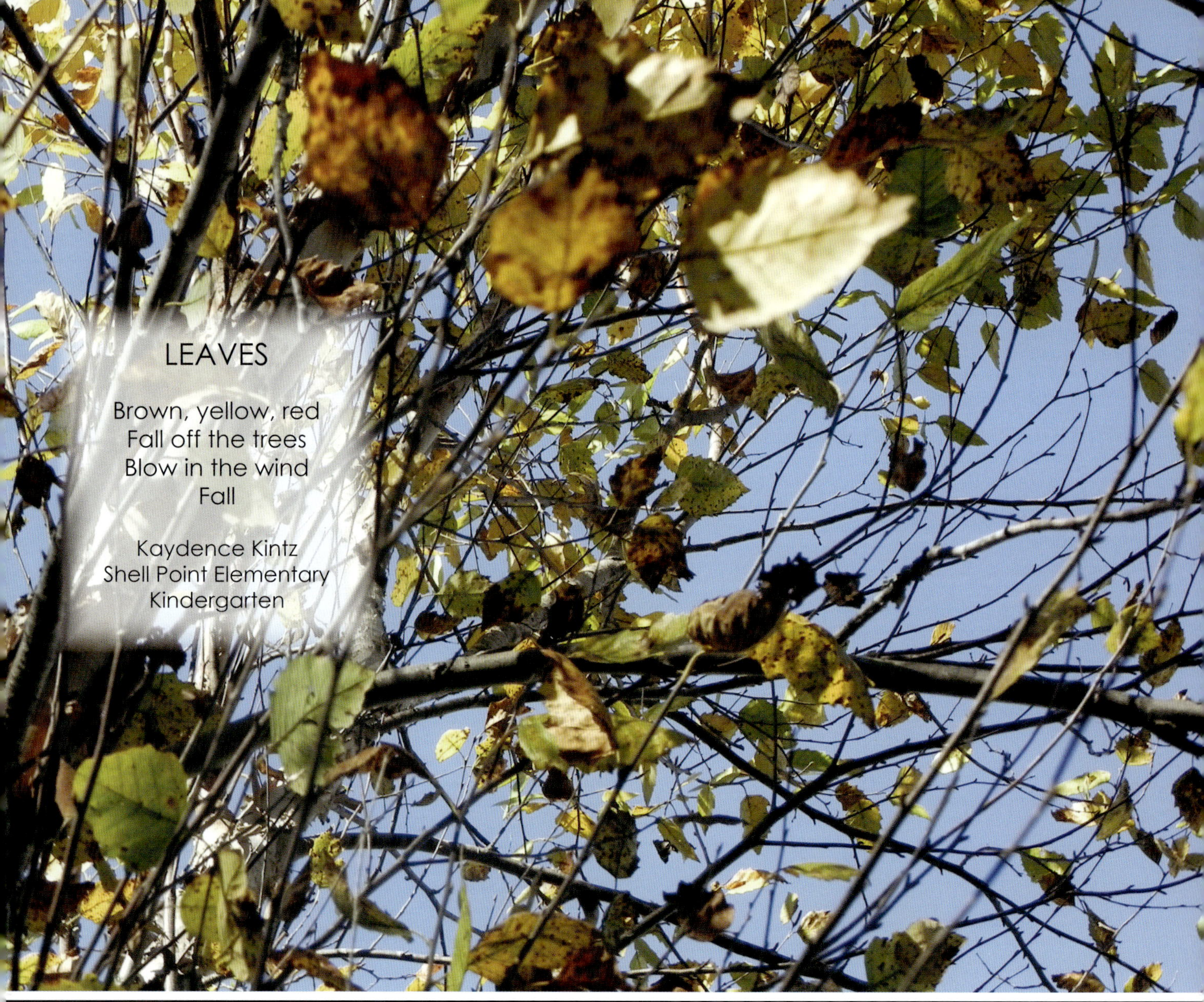

Lily Painton Shell Point Elementary Kindergarten

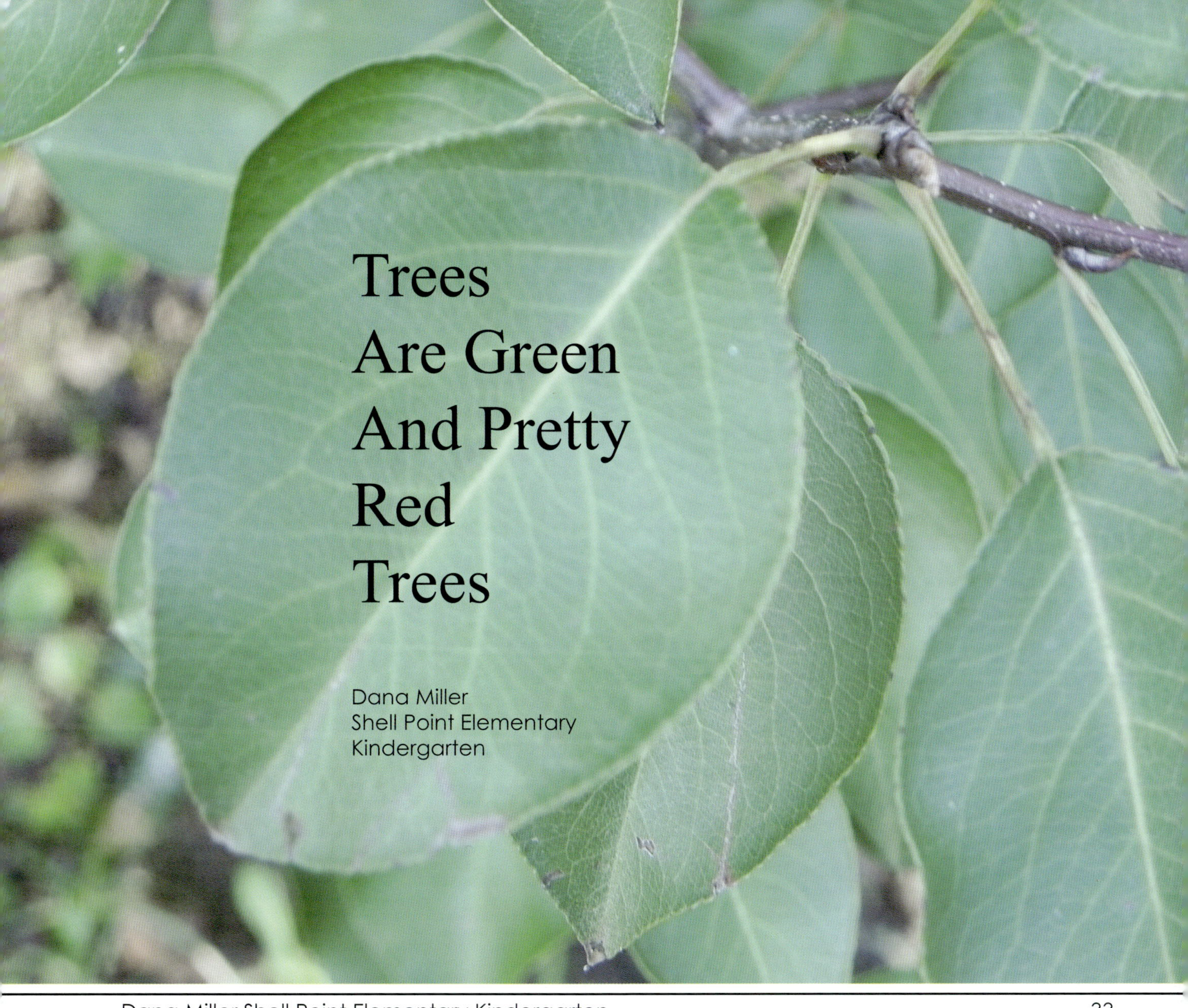
Trees
Are Green
And Pretty

Red

Trees

Dana Miller
Shell Point Elementary
Kindergarten

LOGGERHEAD ADVENTURE

Loggerhead Turtle: swim, swim, swim!
The hard shell upon his back.
The years they age in the sea.
The large amount of young they produce.
Loggerhead Turtle: swim, swim, swim!
Beaks and claws capture prey.
Crabs with hard shells swim away
From the Loggerhead Turtle that wants you today.
In the deep blue sea,
Loggerhead Turtle: swim, swim, swim!

Sierra Jensen
H.E. McCracken Middle
8th Grade

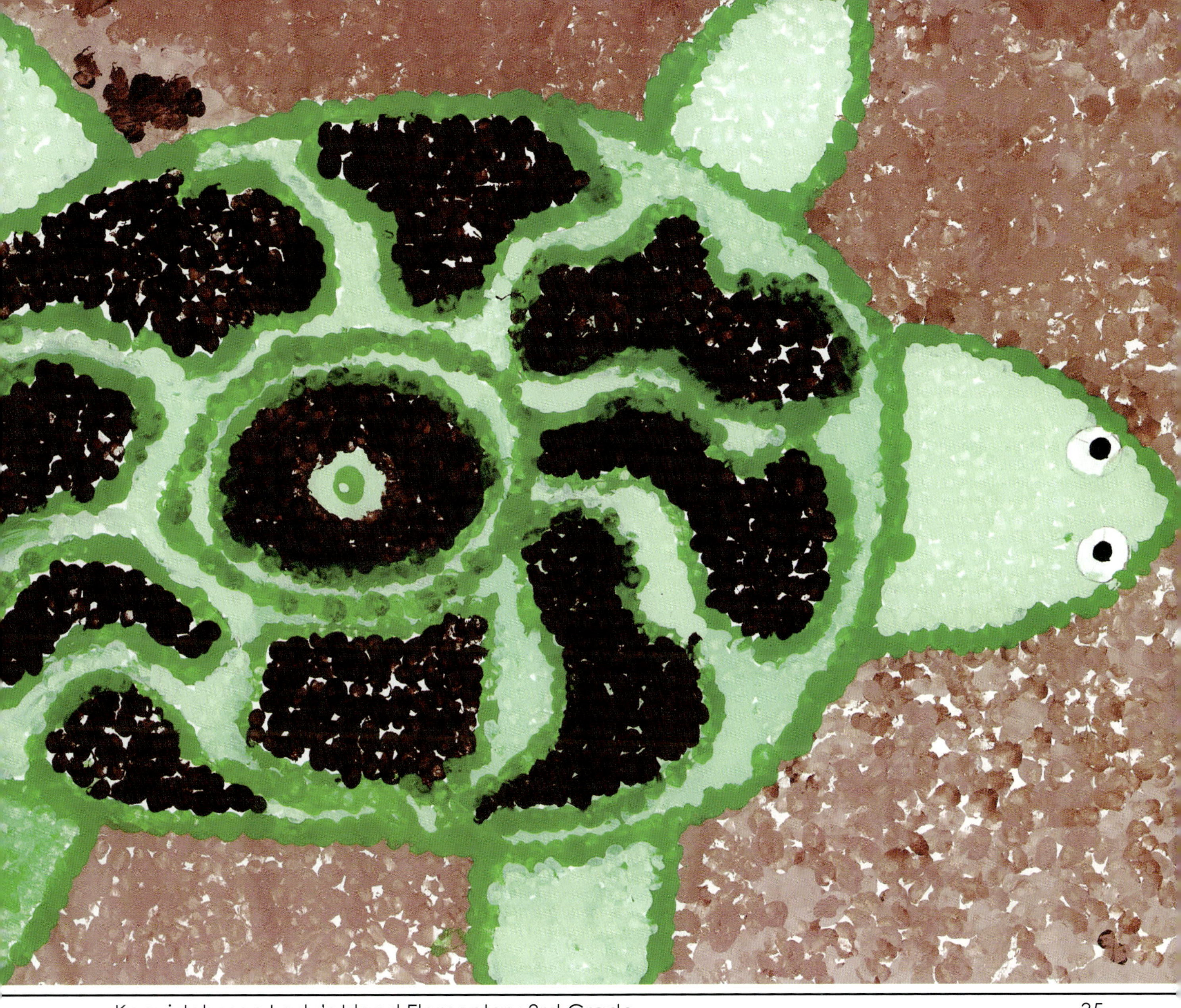

LONELY TREE

I am a lonely tree
Sitting in the daylight
Drying in the sun, washed by the beach
Falling piece by piece
I am a lonely tree

Where can I go?
I have no land
The water swooped it away
I am a lonely tree

These barnacles that coat me
They stay and keep coming
Alas, I am a lonely tree

The water, as long and endless as space
My life such a waste
I am a lonely tree

Will Bootle
Beaufort Middle
7th Grade

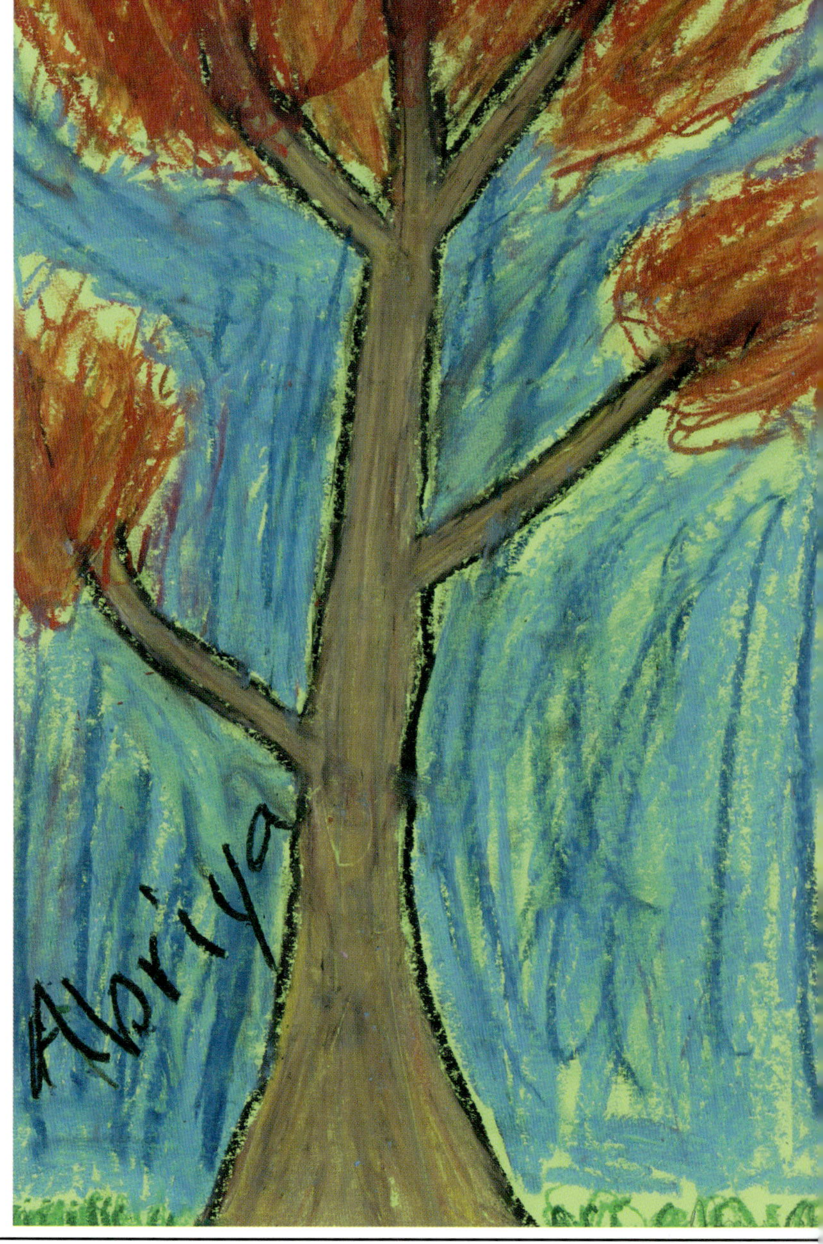

Abriya Hart Pritchardville Elementary 5th Grade

MARITIME

By the sea, water flows on my feet
While a forest sits behind me.
Gabby walks upon the shells.
I watch and wonder.
As waves get bigger, almost to the sky
It makes me want to hide somewhere nearby.

Willie Jones
Robert Smalls Middle
7th Grade

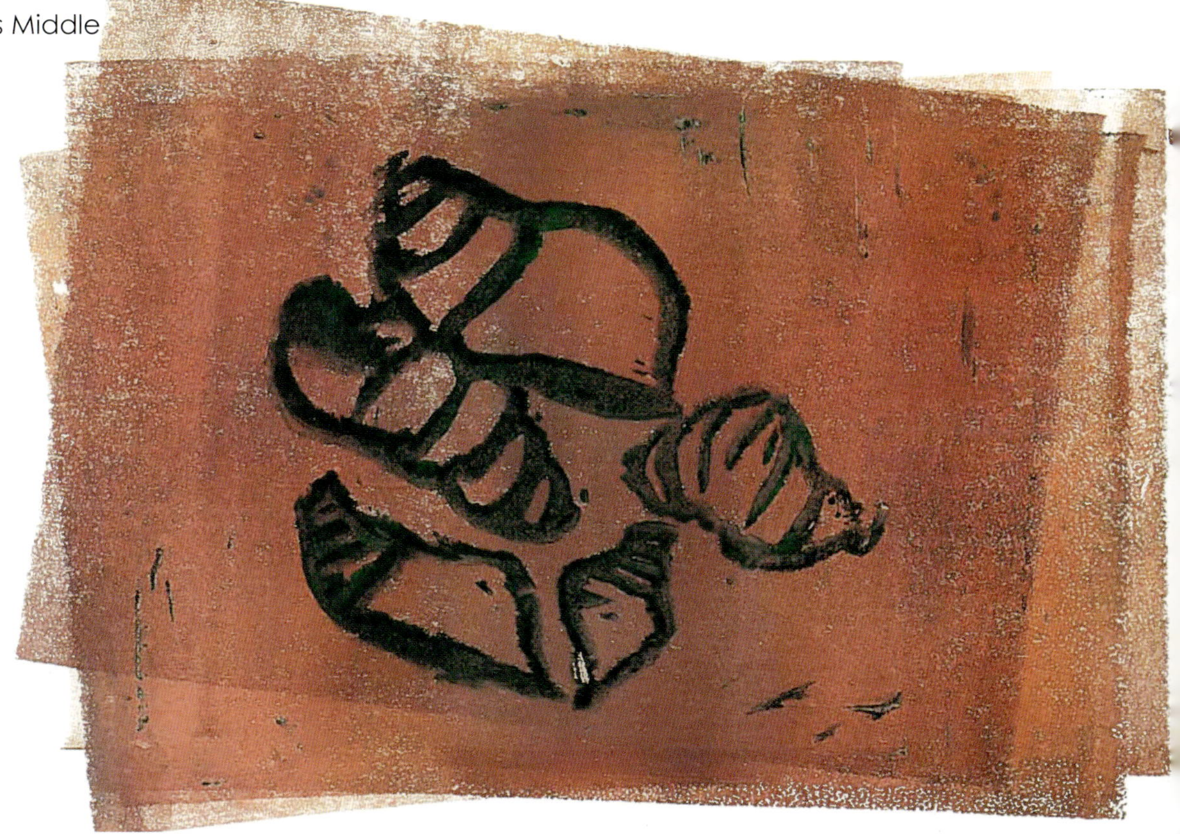

MARKS IN THE SAND

Water waving forever
Over and over the sand
Imprinted in it is a footprint
Symbolizing your mark on the world
Like pebbles ground to powder
Soft ash is the sand
Marked on the beach 'til the tides come
Numerous bits of shells
As big as the world may take it
Kiss the sand, as the water hugs it
This mark... Just balancing perfection

McKenzie Wunder
Beaufort Middle
7th Grade

Summer Phillips Beaufort Middle 8th Grade

HOOKED

Stalk the fish.
Get ready
Go.
Slice through
The water.
 I burst off

The start.
 I chase.
 Flying through
Port Royal Sound.   Stop
 Bite something   sharp! Shut.
 No! It's a hook!   Caught
 And gaffed   into a cooler.
          Lured into Death.

Benjamin Traud
H.E. McCracken Middle
8th Grade

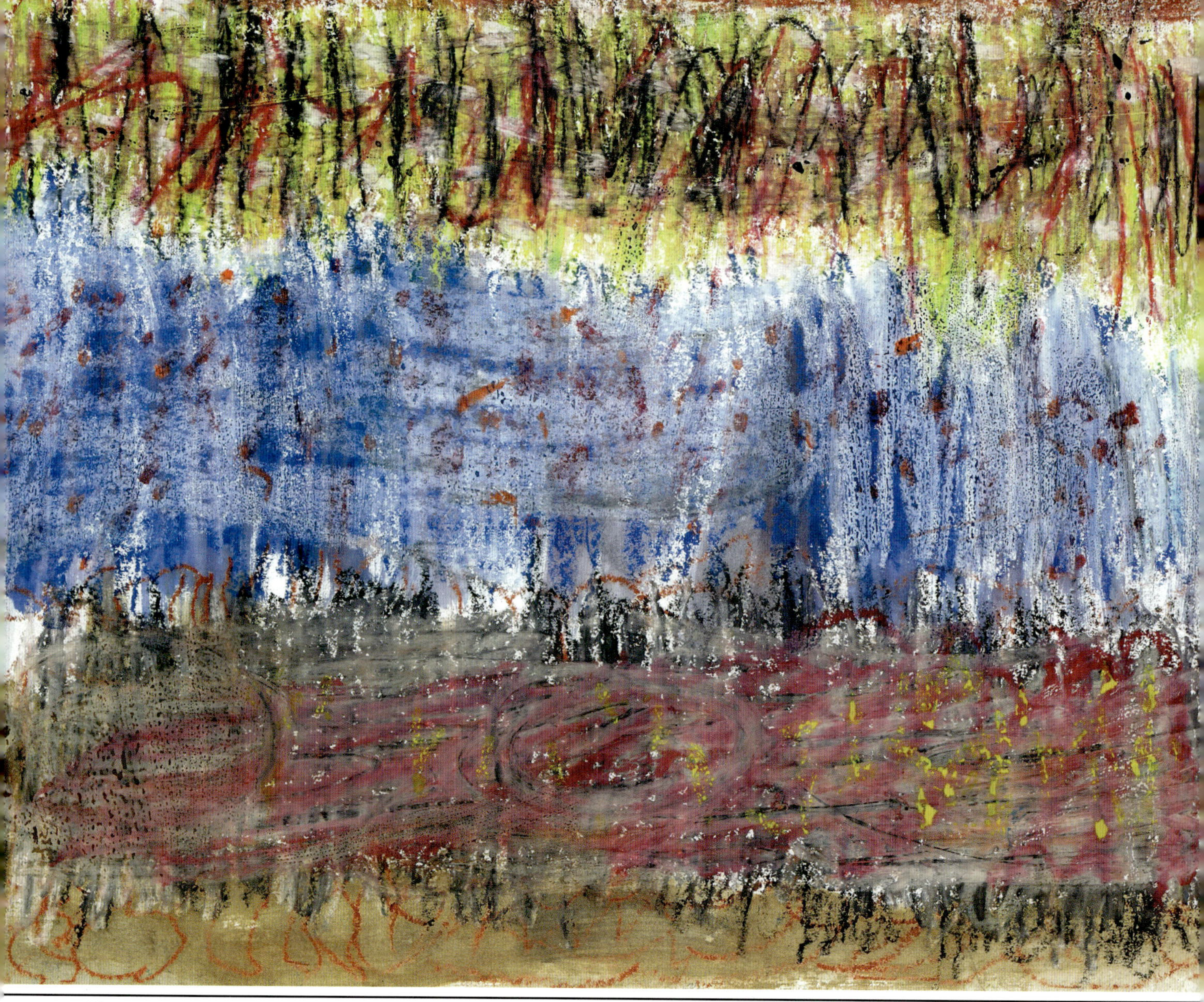

Samantha Soriano Hilton Head Island Elementary 3rd Grade

MARSH

Once walking in puff mud
Small crabs wandered across my feet.
Spartina grass swayed in the wind.
Tiny puddles held fish and algae.
Heron left footprints in the mud.
Dolphins jumped in the air.
So cold.
The sun set
And it was time to go.

Aralyn Townsend
Beaufort Middle
8th Grade

MY CRAB LIFE

Something scared me
AHHHHHHHHHHH!
Is he trying to pick me up?
I don't like this
I hate this
Am I safe?
Quickly, quickly
run in the hole!

DeQuan Griswold
Joseph S. Shanklin Elementary
4th Grade

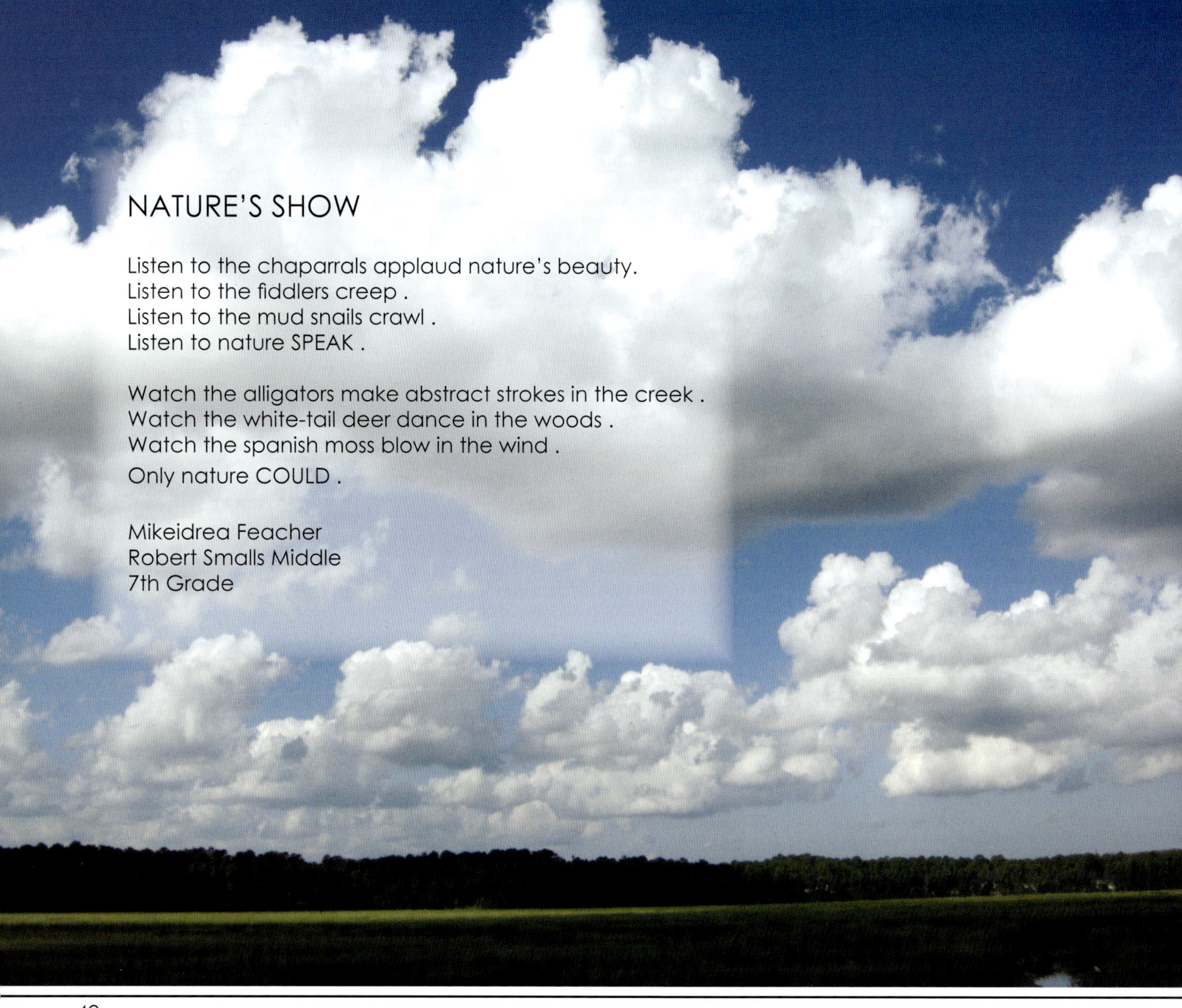

NATURE'S SHOW

Listen to the chaparrals applaud nature's beauty.
Listen to the fiddlers creep .
Listen to the mud snails crawl .
Listen to nature SPEAK .

Watch the alligators make abstract strokes in the creek .
Watch the white-tail deer dance in the woods .
Watch the spanish moss blow in the wind .
Only nature COULD .

Mikeidrea Feacher
Robert Smalls Middle
7th Grade

NATURE'S COMFORT

Jellyfish gliding against the current,
Hanging out,
Breathing so hard,
Their tentacles moving along with the
Current,
Like it is a different animal.

The cold crisp air,
Gliding along the tide,
And getting colder,
Every second, of every minute.

Egrets huddling
Trying to get warm
For their long winter's nap,
While the heron
Cries for help.

Crabs buried so hard, so cold,
For so long
In their crab holes.
Some searching for food,
But having no luck.

Water like glass,
Dark in places, light in others,
Water so strong
It carries the driftwood
To who knows where?

Strange shadows
Wander in the distance,
Coming closer, closer.
A cat sneaking around
Trying not to be seen.

Katie Dyer
Pritchardville Elementary
5th Grade

LIVE OAK

A stationary beginning

Representing hope. Gradually maturing

While standing tall and confident. A symbol of

Strength and dependability, providing a canopy of shelter. A sincere,

Trustworthy friend, with leaves swaying gently, whispering tone of wisdom

To all. Truly an omniscient wonder and delight of graceful beauty and longevity,

Adorned with swooping Spanish moss, telling stories of yester-year. Lovely in stature

Bearing acorns

As fruit. A

Magnificent

Masterpiece

Of nature.

Anna Caroline Cribb
Bluffton Middle
7th Grade

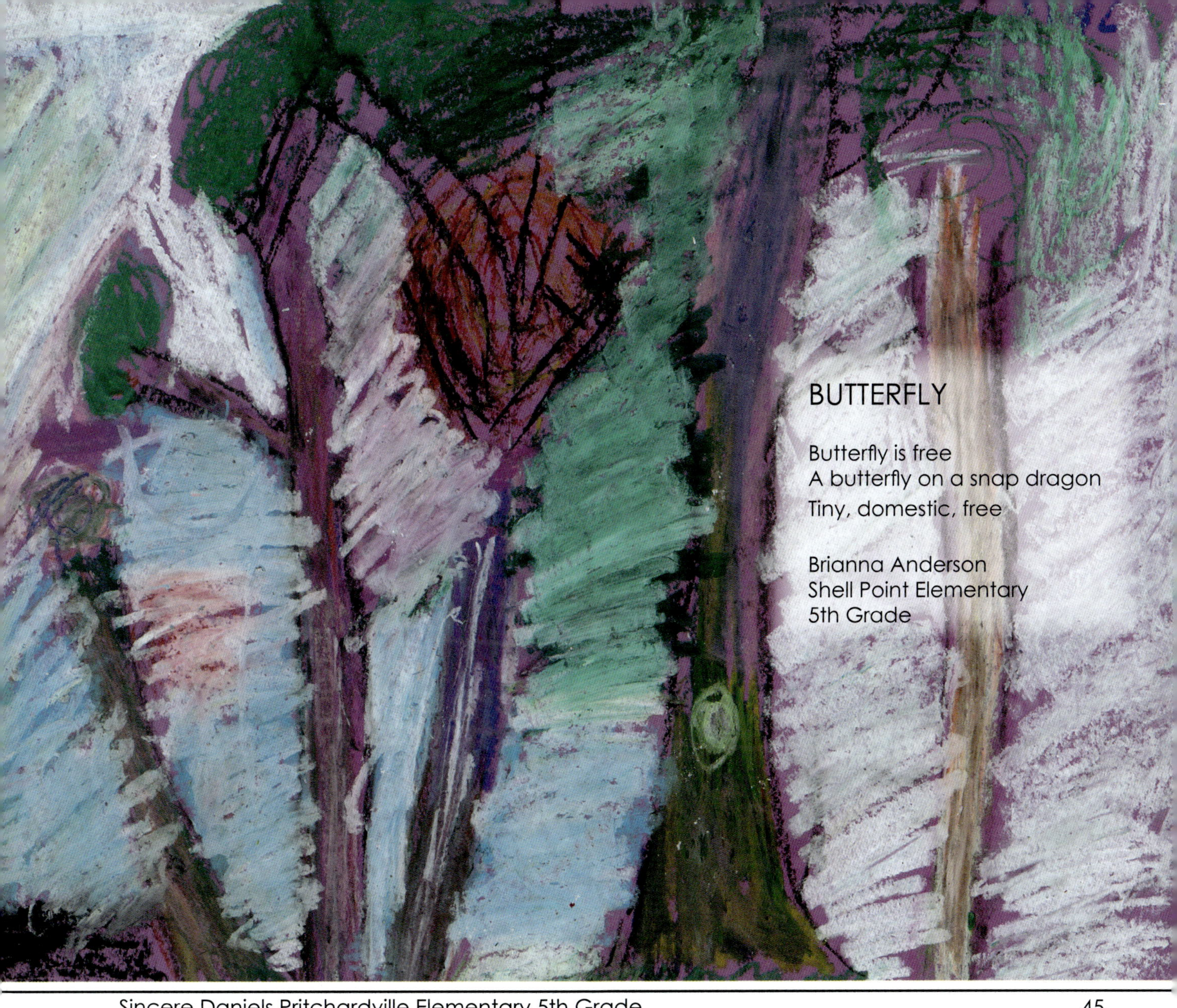
BUTTERFLY

Butterfly is free
A butterfly on a snap dragon
Tiny, domestic, free

Brianna Anderson
Shell Point Elementary
5th Grade

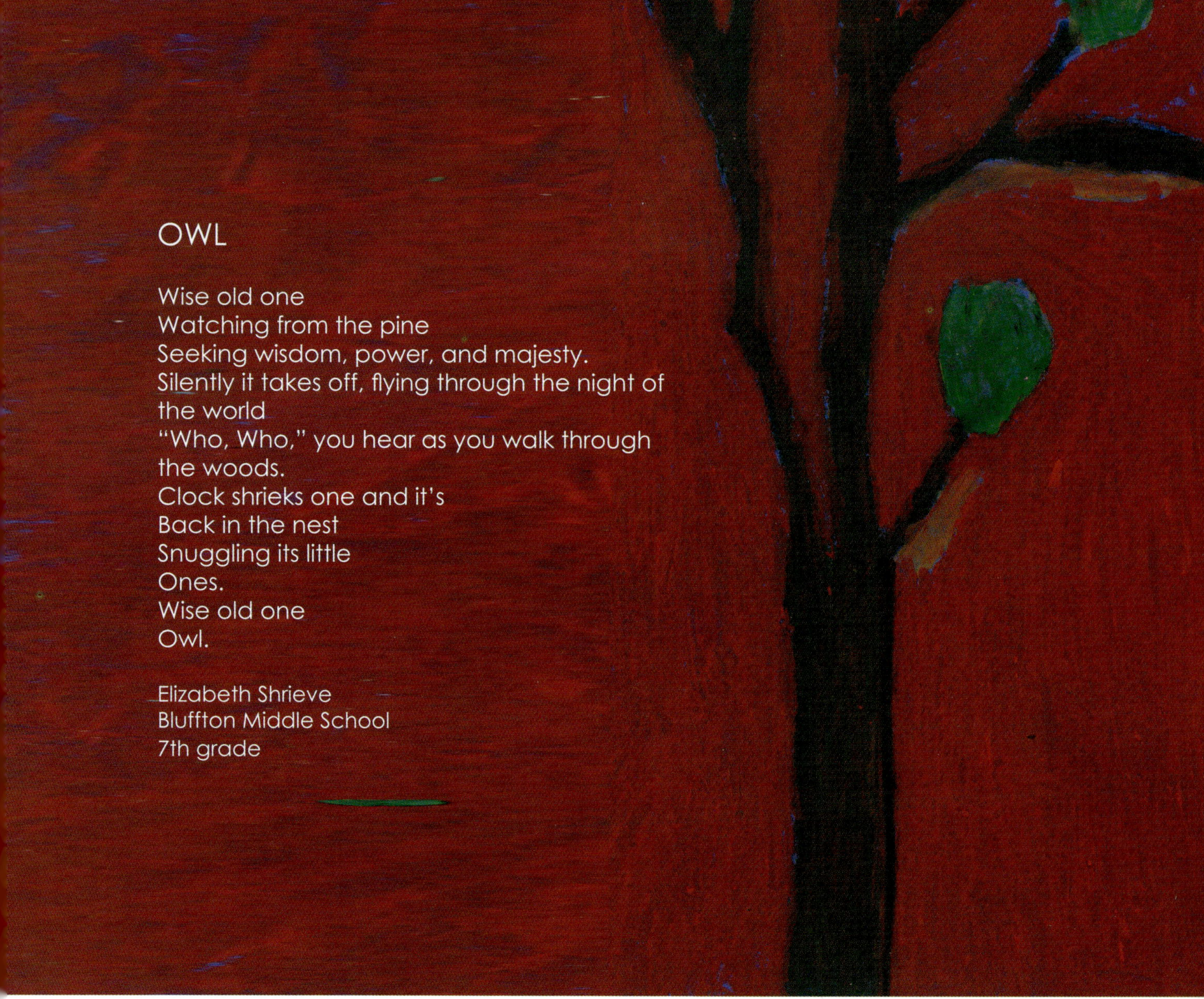

Cameron White Pritchardville Elementary 5th Grade

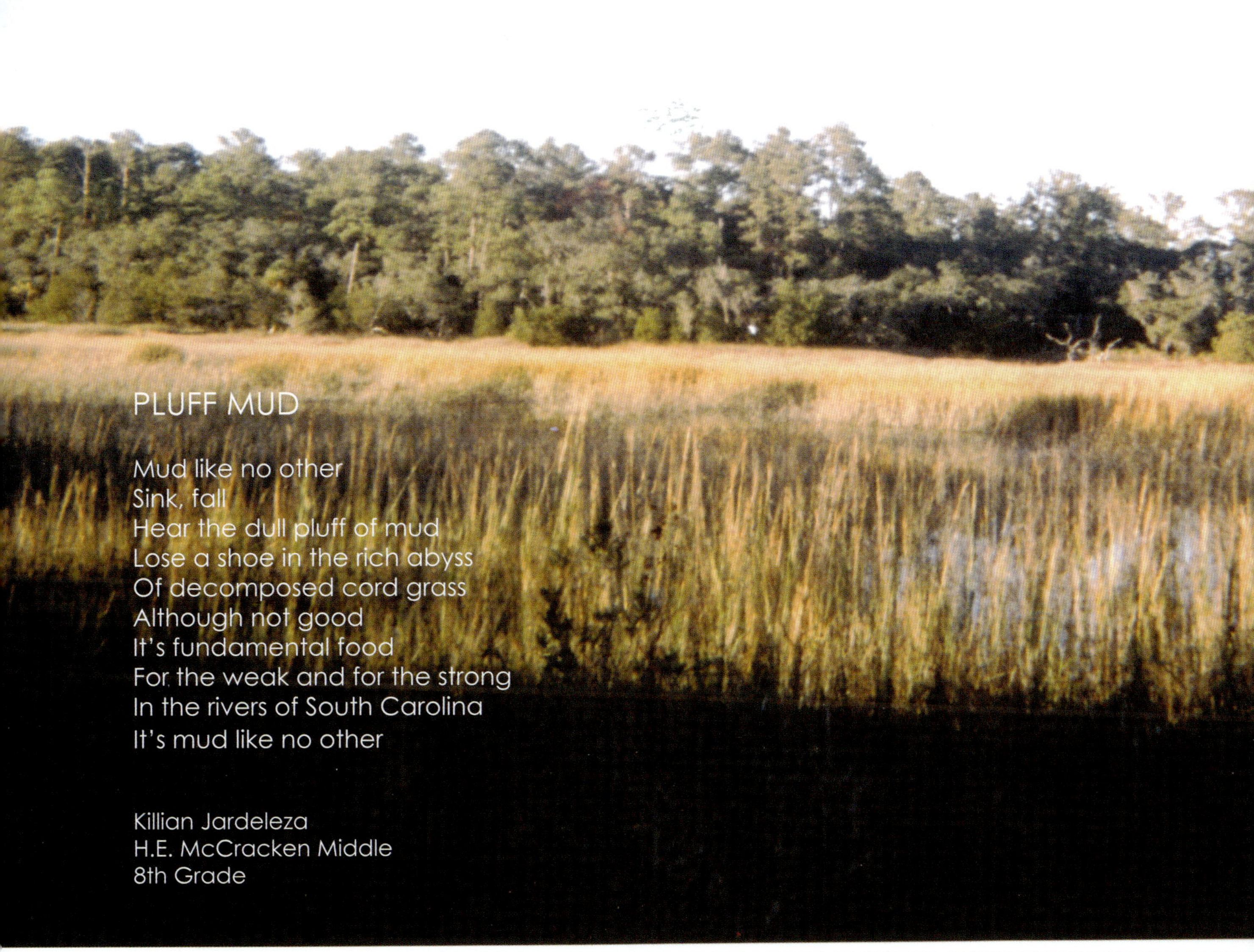

PLUFF MUD

Mud like no other
Sink, fall
Hear the dull pluff of mud
Lose a shoe in the rich abyss
Of decomposed cord grass
Although not good
It's fundamental food
For the weak and for the strong
In the rivers of South Carolina
It's mud like no other

Killian Jardeleza
H.E. McCracken Middle
8th Grade

REMEMBERING THE OCEAN

I remember the burning of my eyes,
from your salted ocean water.
I remember the itching of my skin,
from your yellowish gritty sand.
I remember the screeching of the seagulls,
as they called to one another.
I remember the laughter of family and friends,
and the love for every woman and man.

Paliete Sharpe
Whale Branch Middle
8th Grade

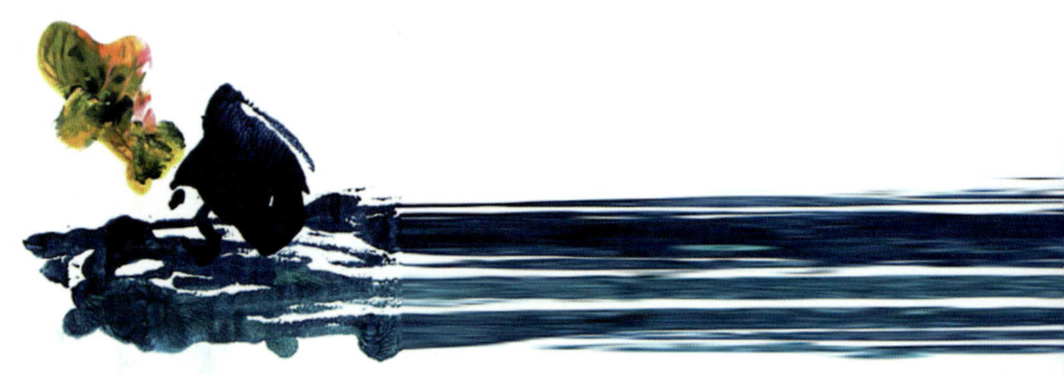

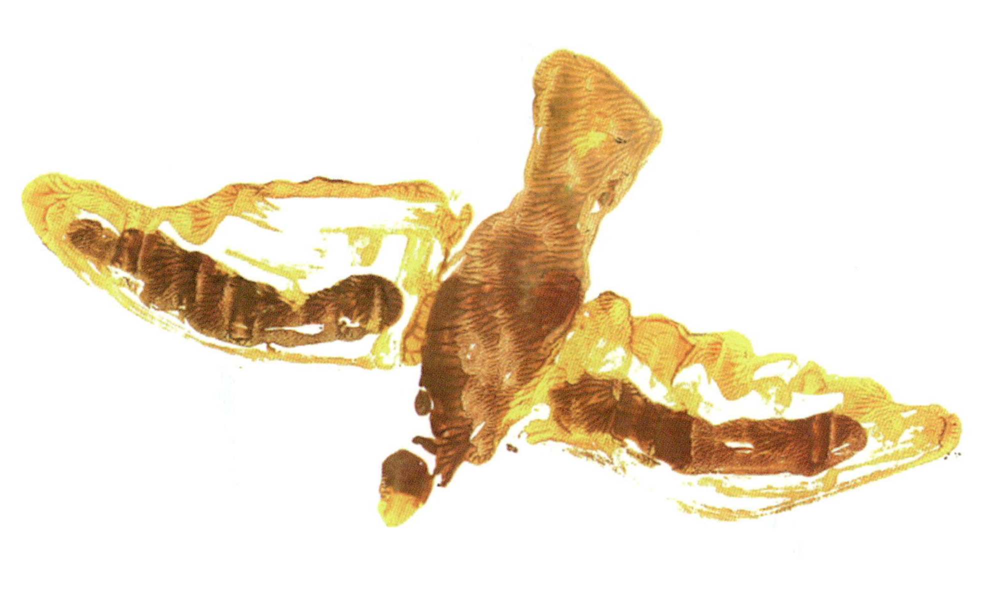

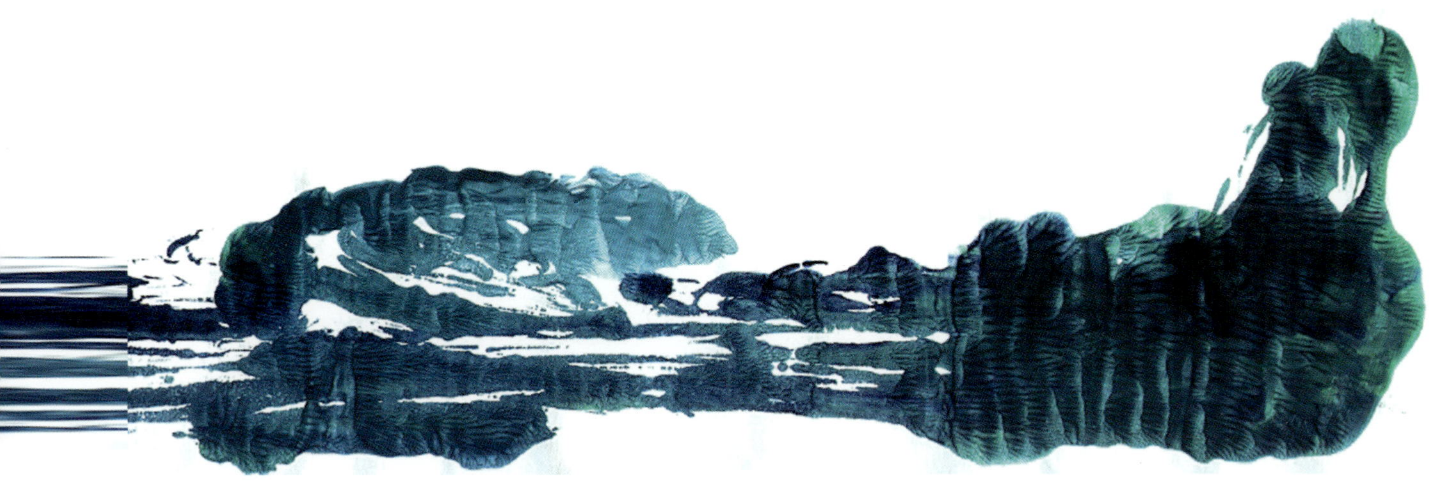

SOUTHERN RIVER
Runoff rain
Rush through the drain
Ends up in me.
I'm starting
TO DIE.
My friends that live in me
Are starting to go away.
Soon I might be alone
With no one.
I'm starting to lose my dignity.
Without me y'all wouldn't have
Fish, oysters, crabs, and shrimp.
Y'all call me dirty and filthy
But little do you know.
I'm turbid,
Full of zooplankton and phytoplankton,
Full of Life.
My integrity and my spirit are strong
I'm salty.
Fresh free falling water tumbling down from the mountain
I am not.
My origin, my life
Is from the Ocean.
I was born from the
OCEAN.

Sasha-Gaye Brown
HE McCracken Middle
8th Grade

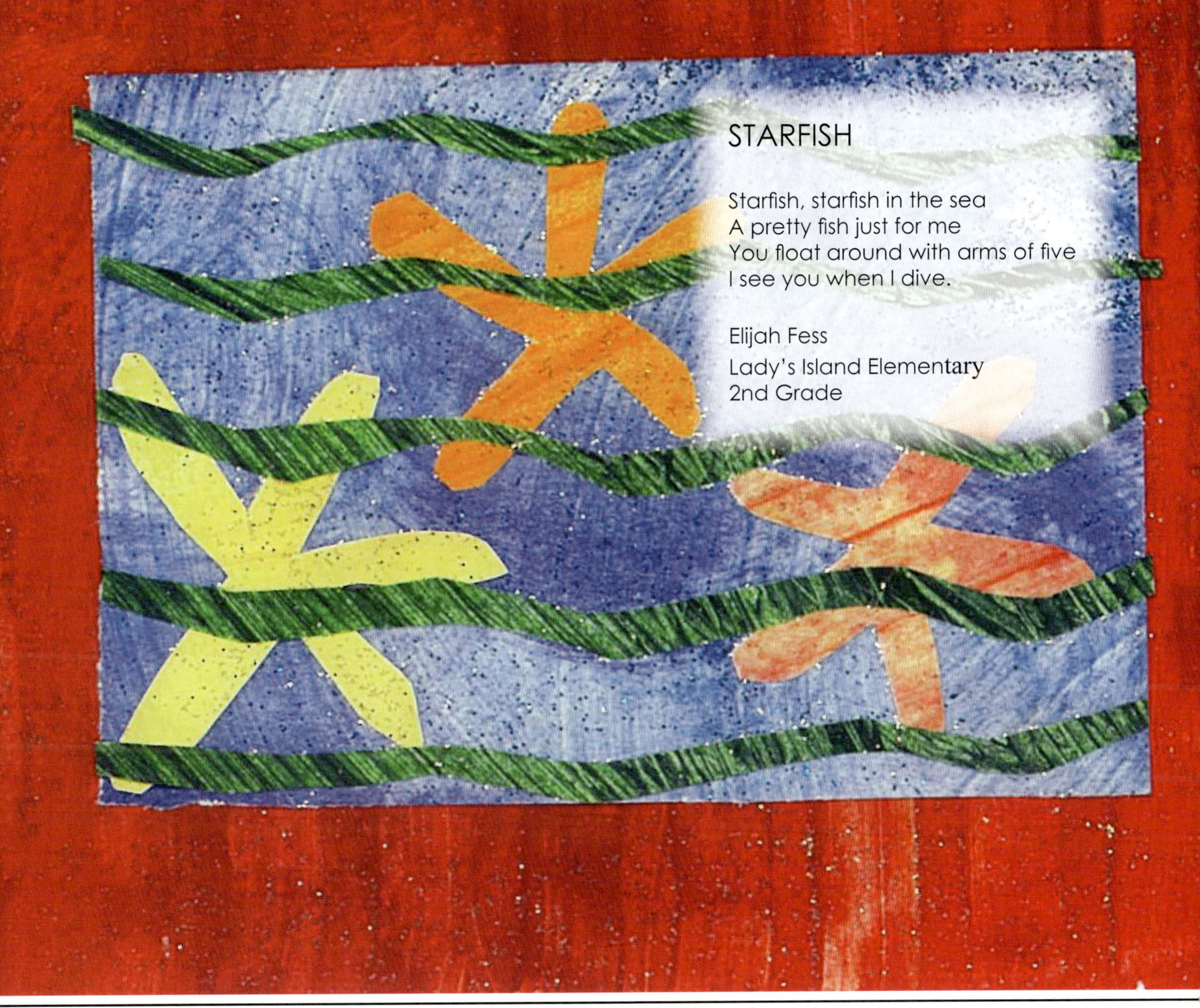

STARFISH

Starfish, starfish in the sea
A pretty fish just for me
You float around with arms of five
I see you when I dive.

Elijah Fess
Lady's Island Elementary
2nd Grade

SPARTINA GRASS

I blow in the wind.
I soak in the water.
I root in the pluff mud.
I withstand nature's worst storms.
I am spartina grass.

Pearce Randal
Robert Smalls Middle
7th Grade

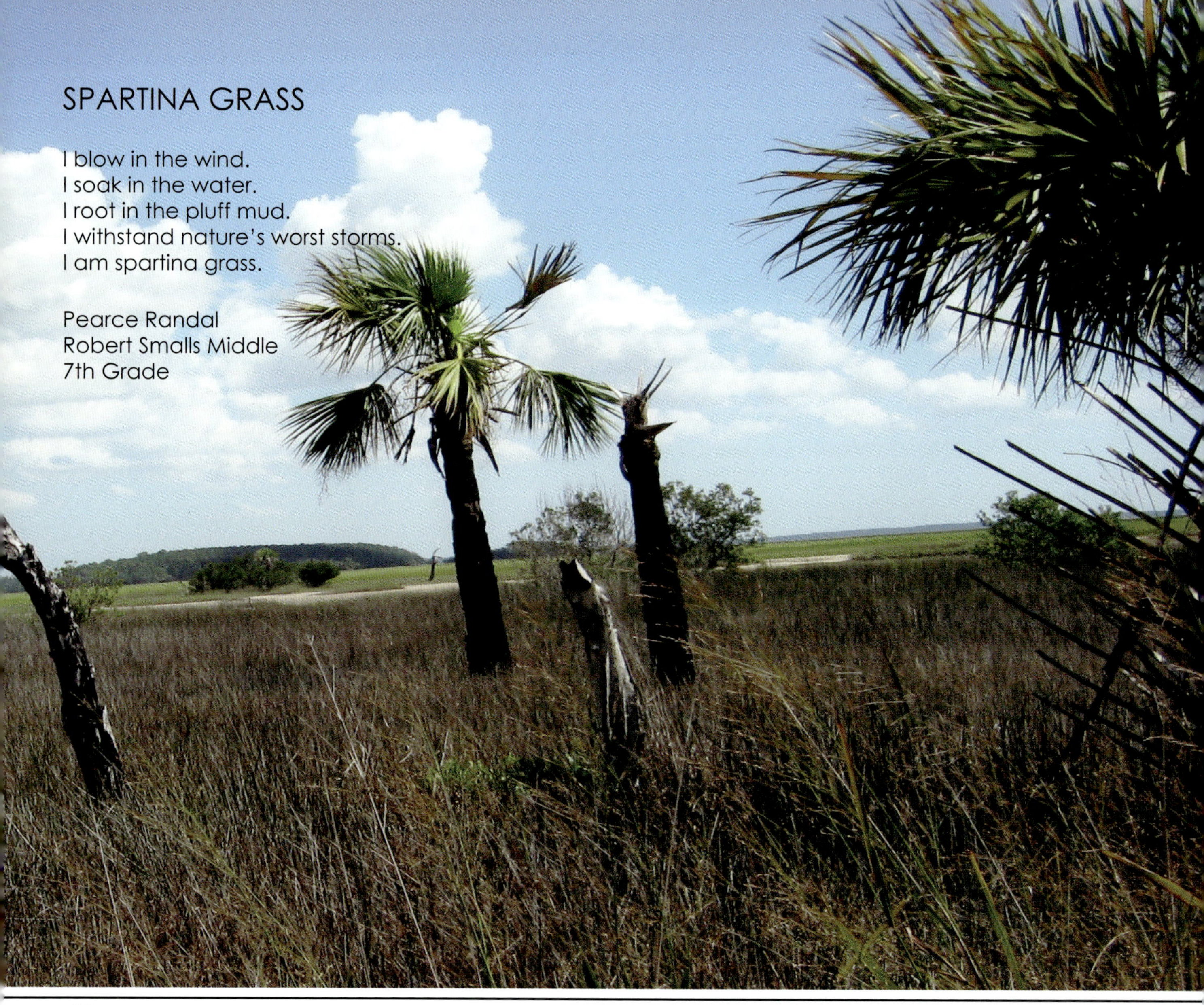

SPARTINA GRASS IN THIS WATERSHED

I, Spartina Grass reside in a salt marsh,
Amidst a Braided stream,
In this watershed,
I am the salt marsh, a natural nursery of brown and green,
Once I was a glorious thing, abundant with minnows, oysters, shrimp, and crab,
Graceful herons used to fly down to fish, their crests held high,
Bottle-nosed dolphins once bounced and skidded across my brackish water,
Singing melodiously to the sky whilst they played,
So it was in the beginning time,
In this watershed,
Before...before...THEM,
Like savage demons they came in their electric vessels,
Maiming the dolphins,
Shooting the herons,
Ravaging my hillocks,
And eating my crabs, my shrimp, my oysters,
In this watershed,
Yet worse carnage was yet to come, far worse,
Pollution, hazardous wastes, were carried by the runoff from the human's impervious
 surfaces,
I, Spartina Grass am apparently the processing plan for these various
abominations,
I fight the battle, but even I must relent,
I feel life slipping away, as if I'm sinking through the detritus,
Giving into eternal sleep,
In...this...watershed.

Spencer McAllister
Bluffton Middle
7th Grade

STILL CATCHLESS

With water like glass
and sticks floating by,
Spanish moss hanging down
like clouds in the sky.
Hunting bird coming up to take a breath,
and going back under
like a promise to be kept,
A rainbow of a jellyfish
wafting with the current,
an endless pattern of grass in the marsh.
The hunting bird comes up again,
waiting for a sign of movement
or noise anticipating lunch…
Still catchless.

Tyler Hundley
Pritchardville Elementary
5th Grade

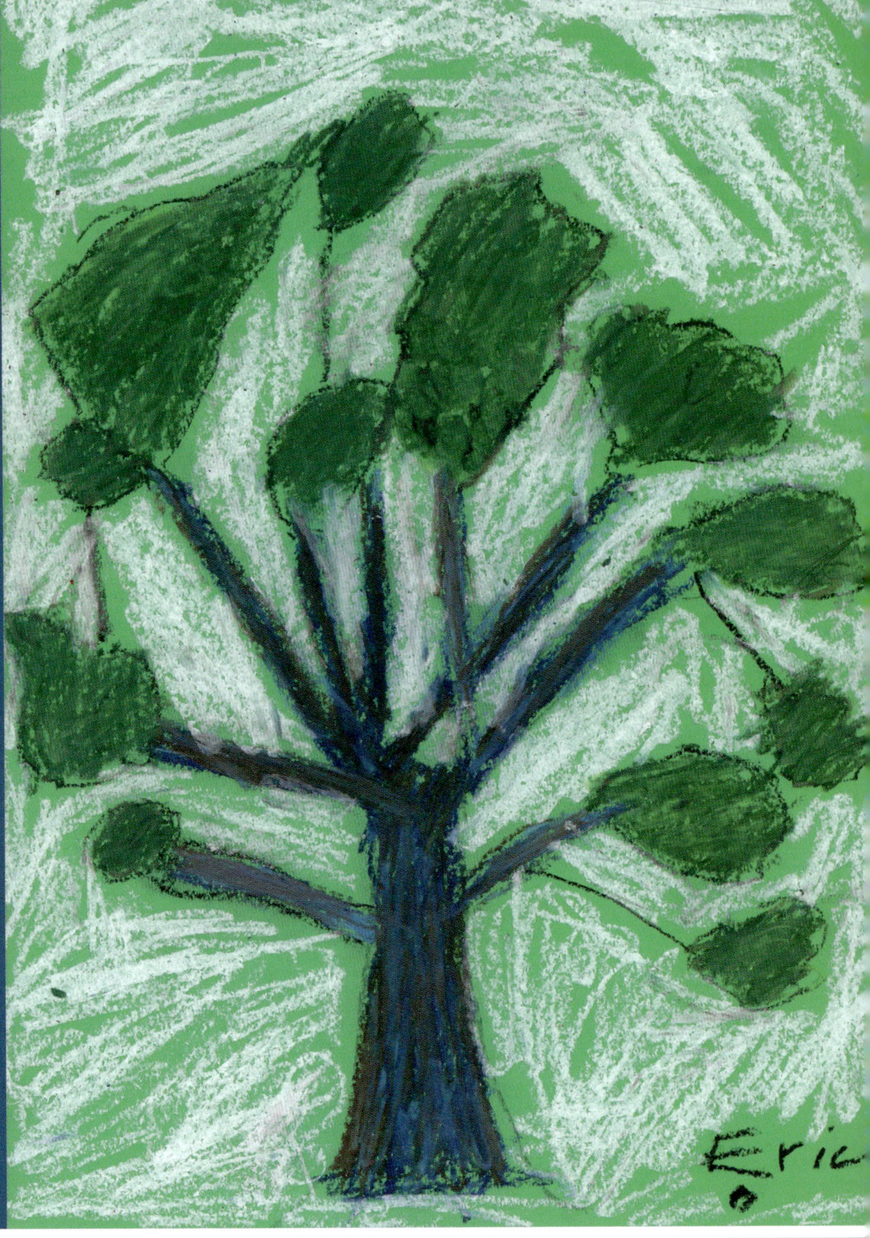

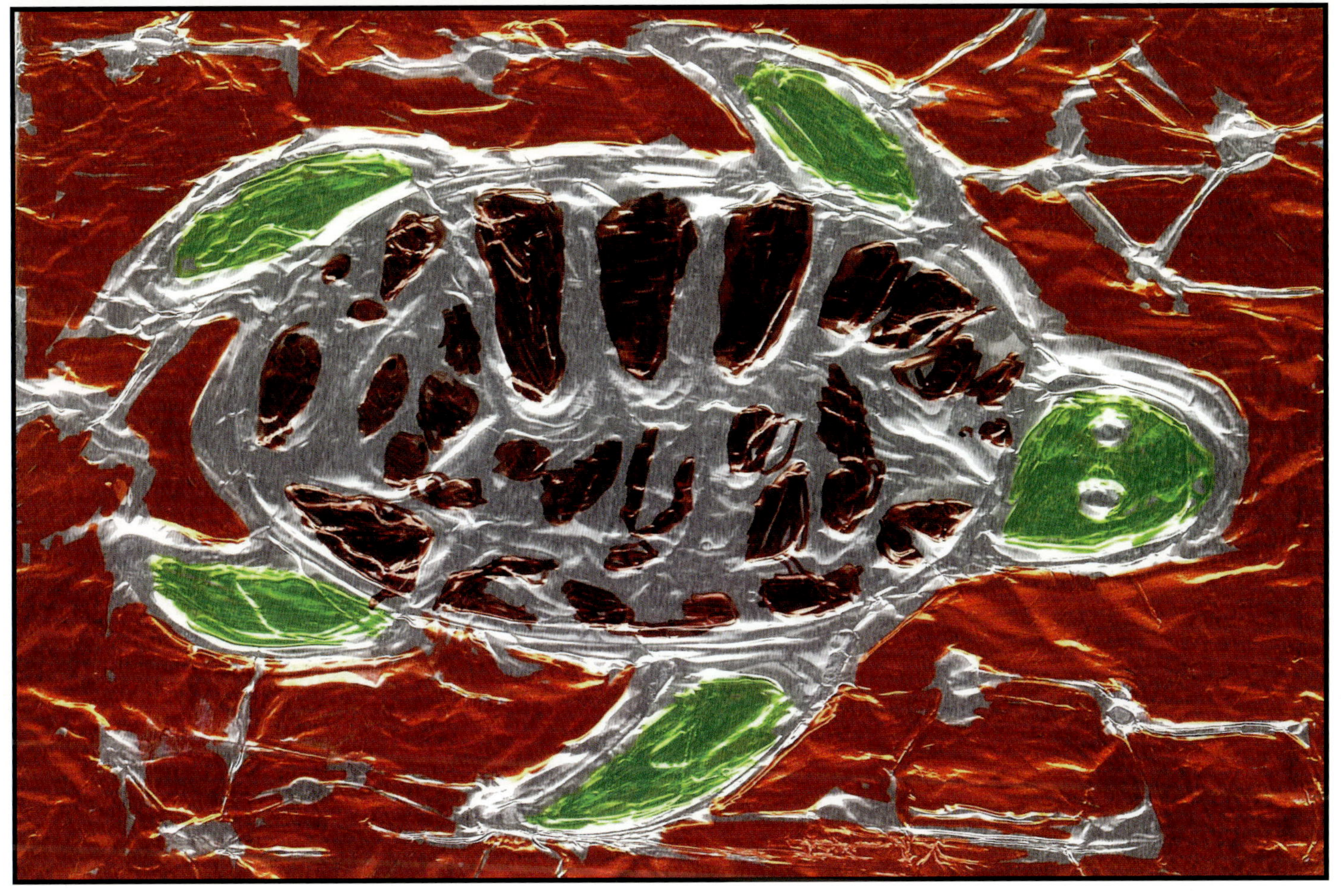

TERRIFIC TURTLE

Terrific turtle leads her sweet babies into the deep blue sea. She is the most beautiful one.
She puts her babies on her back like a little train around the sea.

Jenna Gaskins
Lady's Island Elementary
2nd Grade

THE BEACH

The beach is sand that is warm like a cozy blanket but soft like a cloud.
The beach is kites flying in the air like birds, and then all of a sudden swooping down and getting worms for their babies.
The beach is waves that rock my boogie board up and down like a yoyo.
The beach is bubbles that float through the air like a thousand million butterflies.

Maureen Waunch
Lady's Island Elementary
3rd Grade

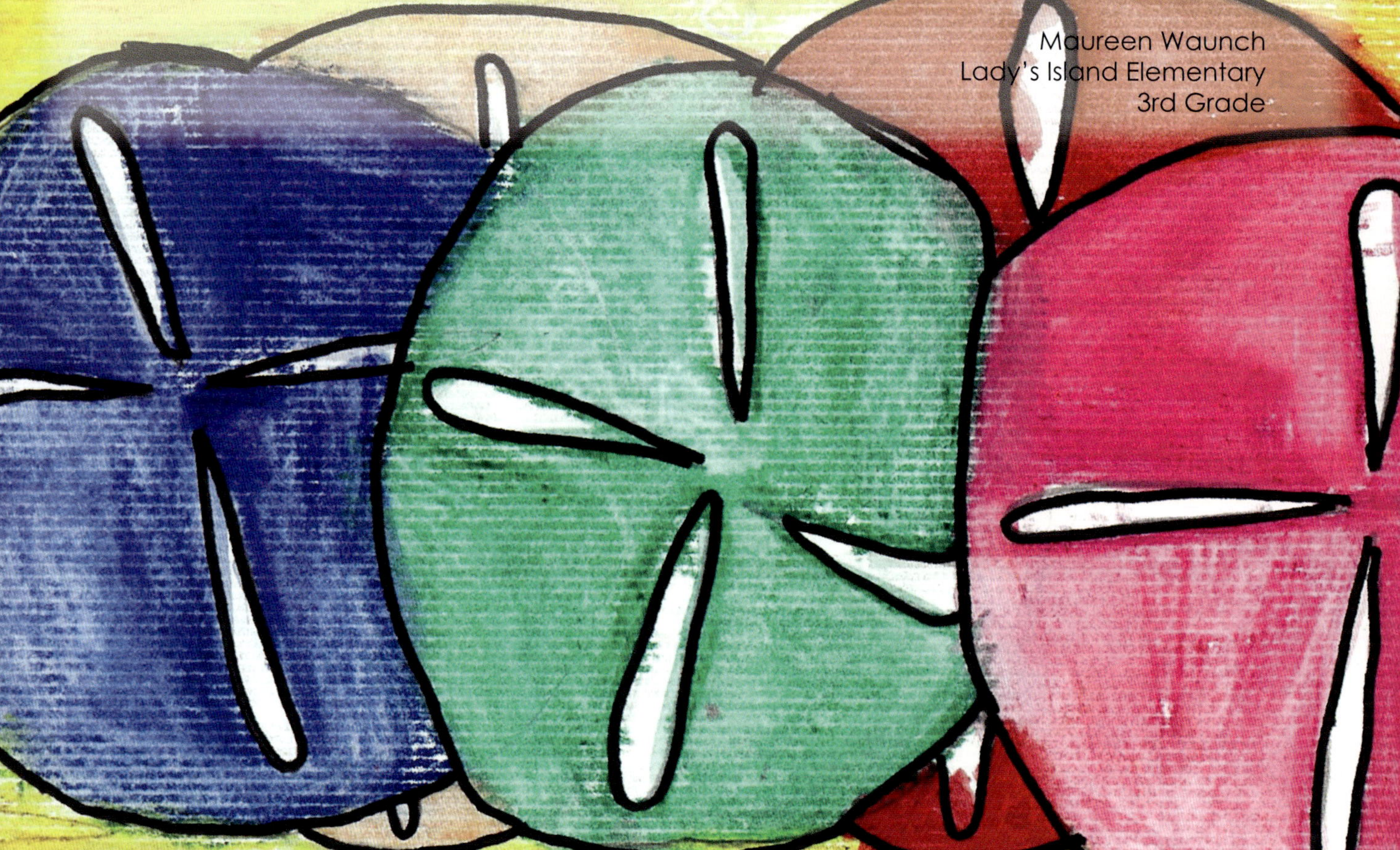

Hailey Boltin Lady's Island Elementary 4th Grade

MONSTER PUFFER FISH

"Ha!Ha! You're ugly!"
It plays in my head like a broken record.
I need anger management,
Well...
That's what everyone says.
Little shrimp think I'm a toy,
Pow! Pow!
They hit me with rocks
Then PUFF!
"Ha! Ha!"Look at the fat man!"
I wish everyone would leave me alone!
I feel like an alien in Times Square.
Everyone is so fascinated with me,
Until...
I BLOW!
Everyone says I'm the Incredible Hulk
Without the incredible.
I just wish,
That everyone would leave me alone!

Uh, oh! Here it goes,
PUFF
PUFF
RUN!

Marrcel Smith
HE McCracken Middle
8th Grade

THE SEA

I love the sea
It's fun to me
The waves are cool
And better than school!

Nolan Savarese
Lady's Island Elementary
2nd Grade

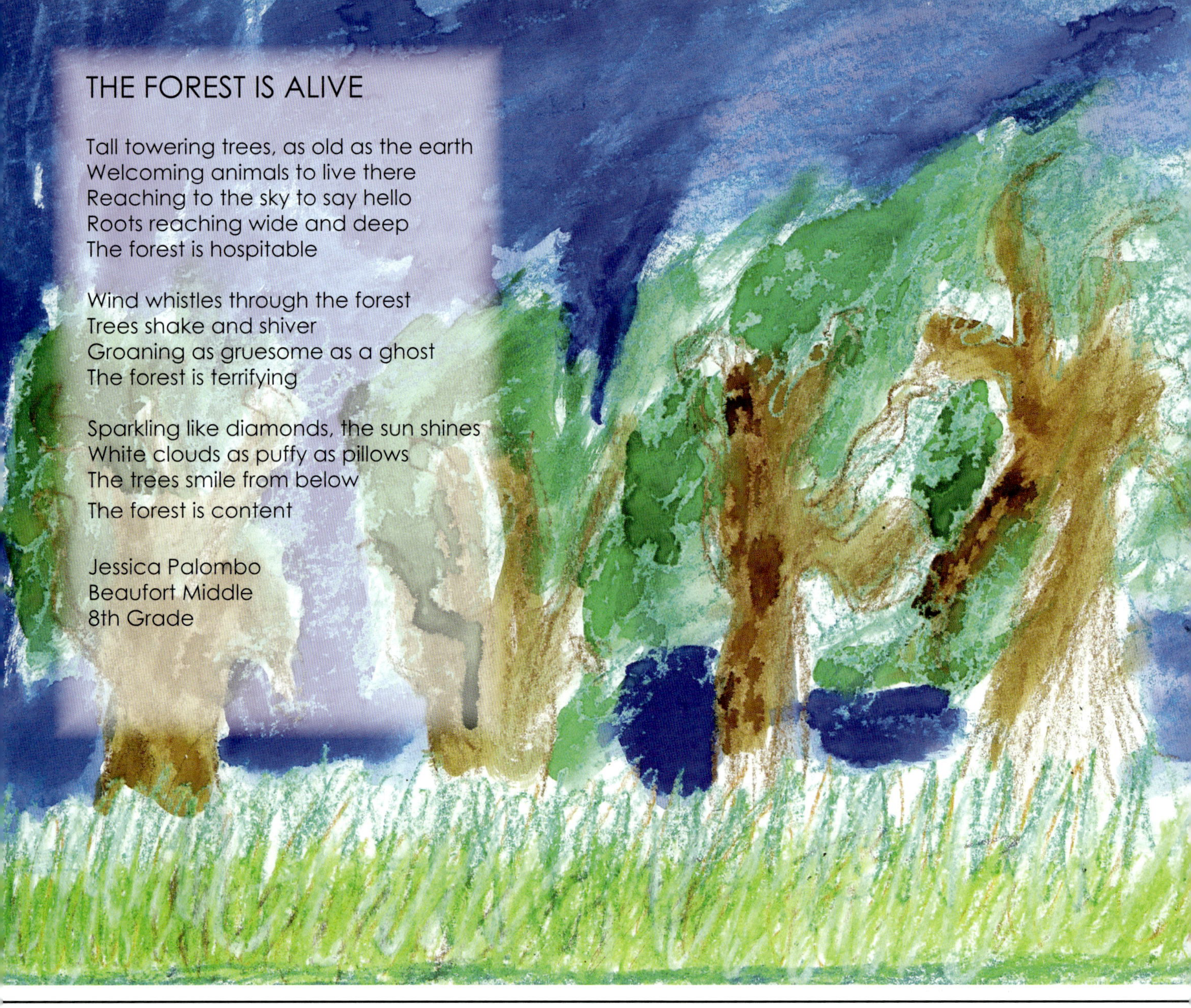

Arnant Aguilar Hilton Head Island Elementary 3rd Grade

THE MARSH

The marsh is where I've spent my time shrimping, swimming, and casting out line
As the seasons change so does she from a gorgeous green to glittering gold
It holds stories of the river untold the marsh hen's call,
The dolphins all memories the marsh holds to keep

Robin Sanders - Beaufort High

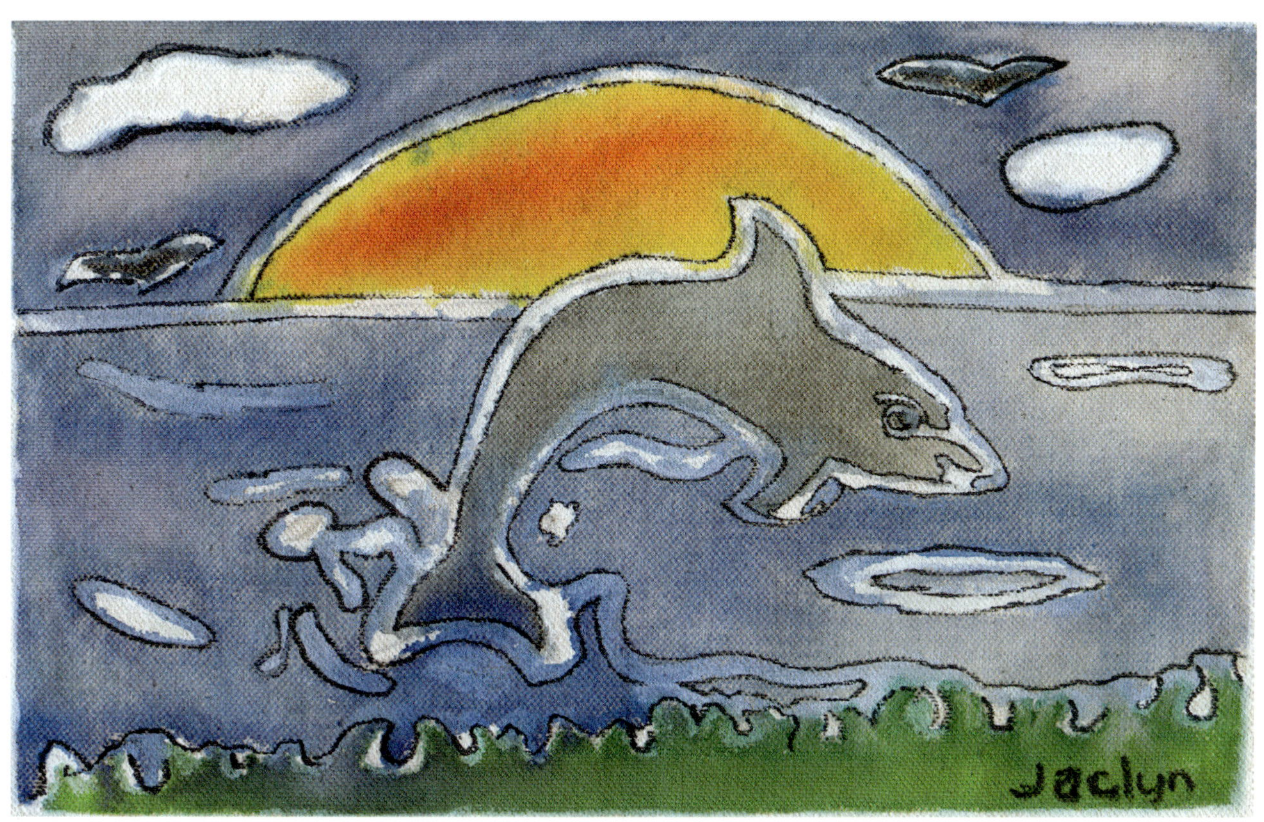

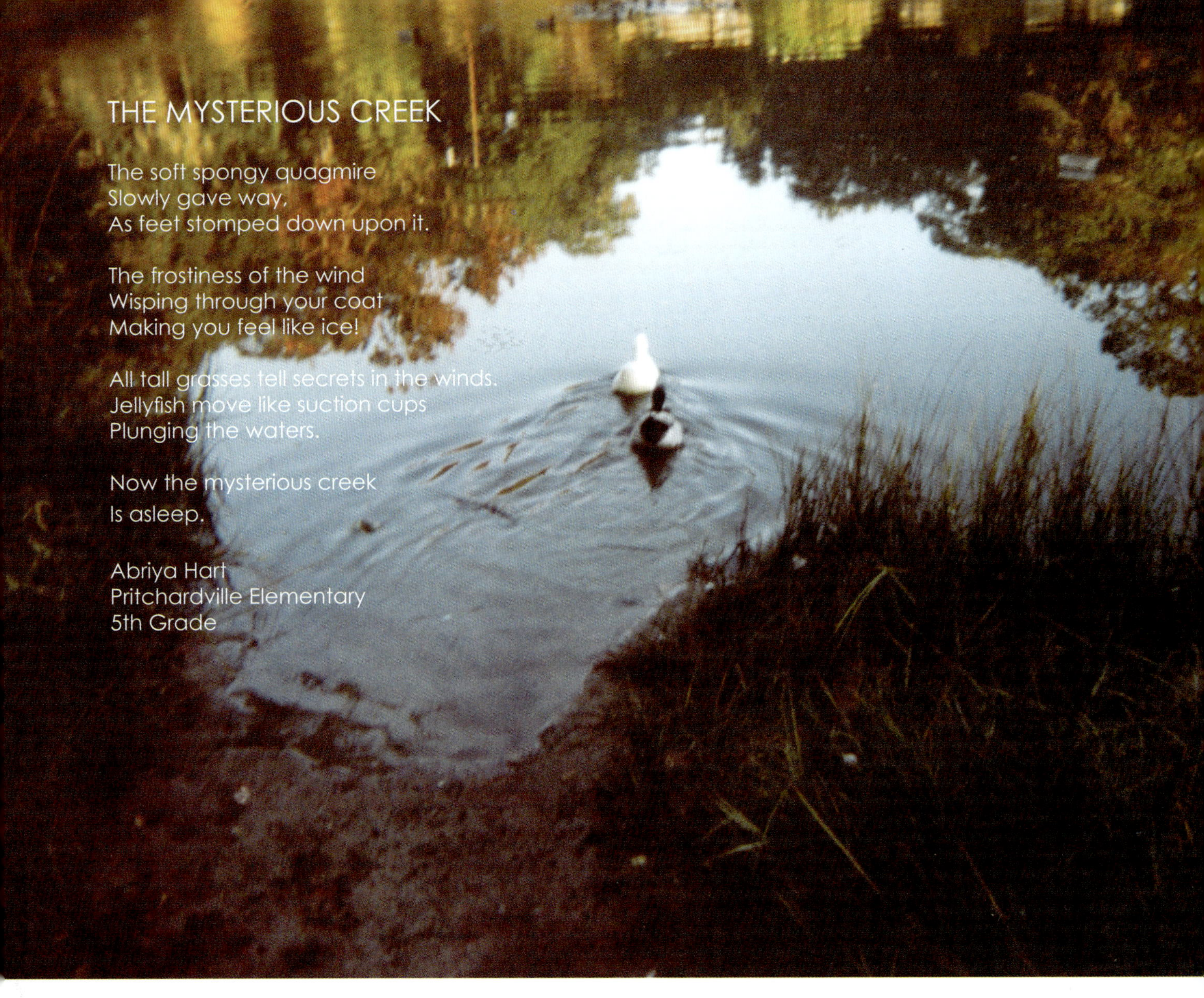

Kori Smith Shell Point Elementary 5th Grade

THICK WET SAND

I'm from cold salty waves lapping at my toes
And eagerly watching lady bugs trail along my fingers
Sitting out in the grass chasing the fluttering wings of butterflies

I'm from Beaufort, South Carolina
Tossing and tipping boat rides on the river
Rolling 'round in the thick, wet sand
And catching our dinner on a hook
I'm from sweet chocolate muffins in my easy bake oven
Nestled in a fort of chairs and sheets held by hair ties
And slipping round on the trampoline after the rain

I'm from strawberries barely clutching the vine
Shaking pears from their high up branches
Dangerous peppers with a fiery heat
And frighteningly beautiful roses in the garden

I'm from the Scheper family
Daughter of Termite
Granddaughter of Willy

I am from casting out my line
Baking warm soft cookies with my mom
Digging a deep dark tunnel in the backyard
Exploring the endless mysterious woods

Rachel Scheper
Beaufort Middle
8th Grade

SQUID

Swimming, swimming all day long,
Each day goes by in a blur.
I go from thing to thing,
Place to place,
I am the target.
I am wanted by other creatures.
My life flashes before my eyes.
Scared
Afraid
Inking
Hiding

Baylee Jacobs
H.E. McCracken Middle School
8th Grade

THINKING

I wake up every morning
Thinking the same thought,
It isn't easy being a shrimp
I am eaten by everything.

I have to dart away
Always moving,
I'm just thankful for my eyes
I can see all around.

When I sleep
I'm always scared,
Thinking that same thought
It isn't easy being a shrimp.

Jordan Scott
H.E. McCracken Middle
8th Grade

THIS IS THE LIFE

Laying in the sand
Feeling the sun beating down on
my back
Mmmmmmhhhhhmmm,
this is the life!

Tress blowing in the cool wind
Reaching the fluffy clouds
Mmmmmmhhhhhmmm,
this is the life!

Hearing the waves crash on the
cool wet sand,
Smelling the salty ocean
Tasting the salty sea pickles
Mmmmmmhhhhhmmm,
this is the life!

Amber Dykeman
Beaufort Middle
7th Grade

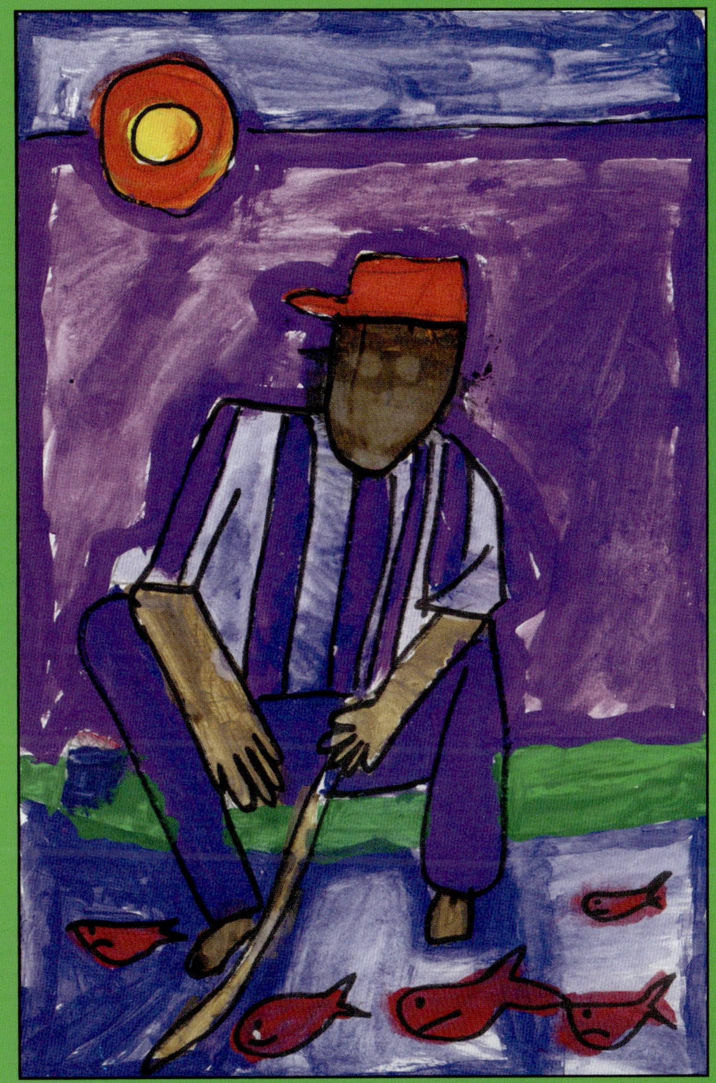

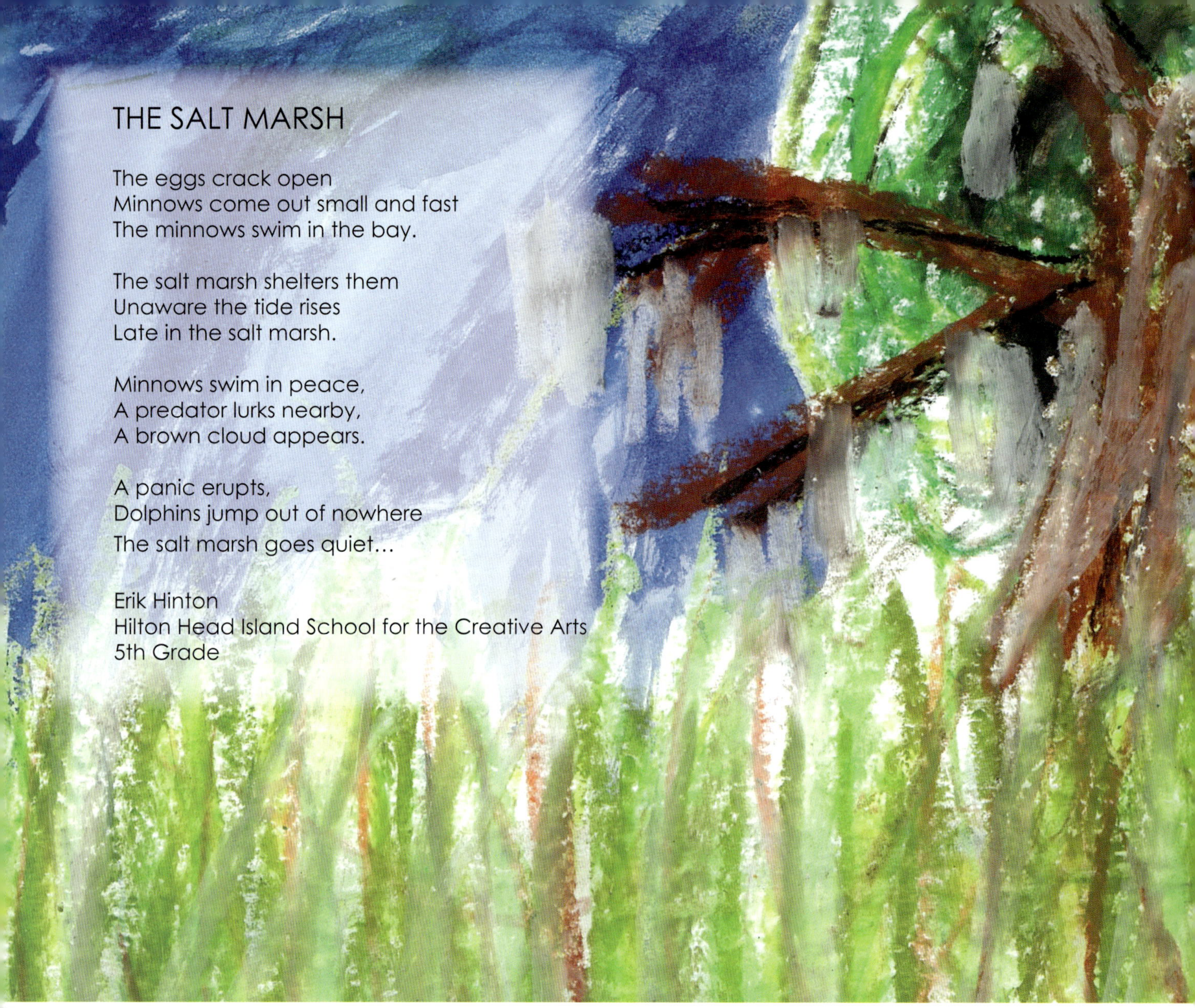

THE SALT MARSH

The eggs crack open
Minnows come out small and fast
The minnows swim in the bay.

The salt marsh shelters them
Unaware the tide rises
Late in the salt marsh.

Minnows swim in peace,
A predator lurks nearby,
A brown cloud appears.

A panic erupts,
Dolphins jump out of nowhere
The salt marsh goes quiet…

Erik Hinton
Hilton Head Island School for the Creative Arts
5th Grade

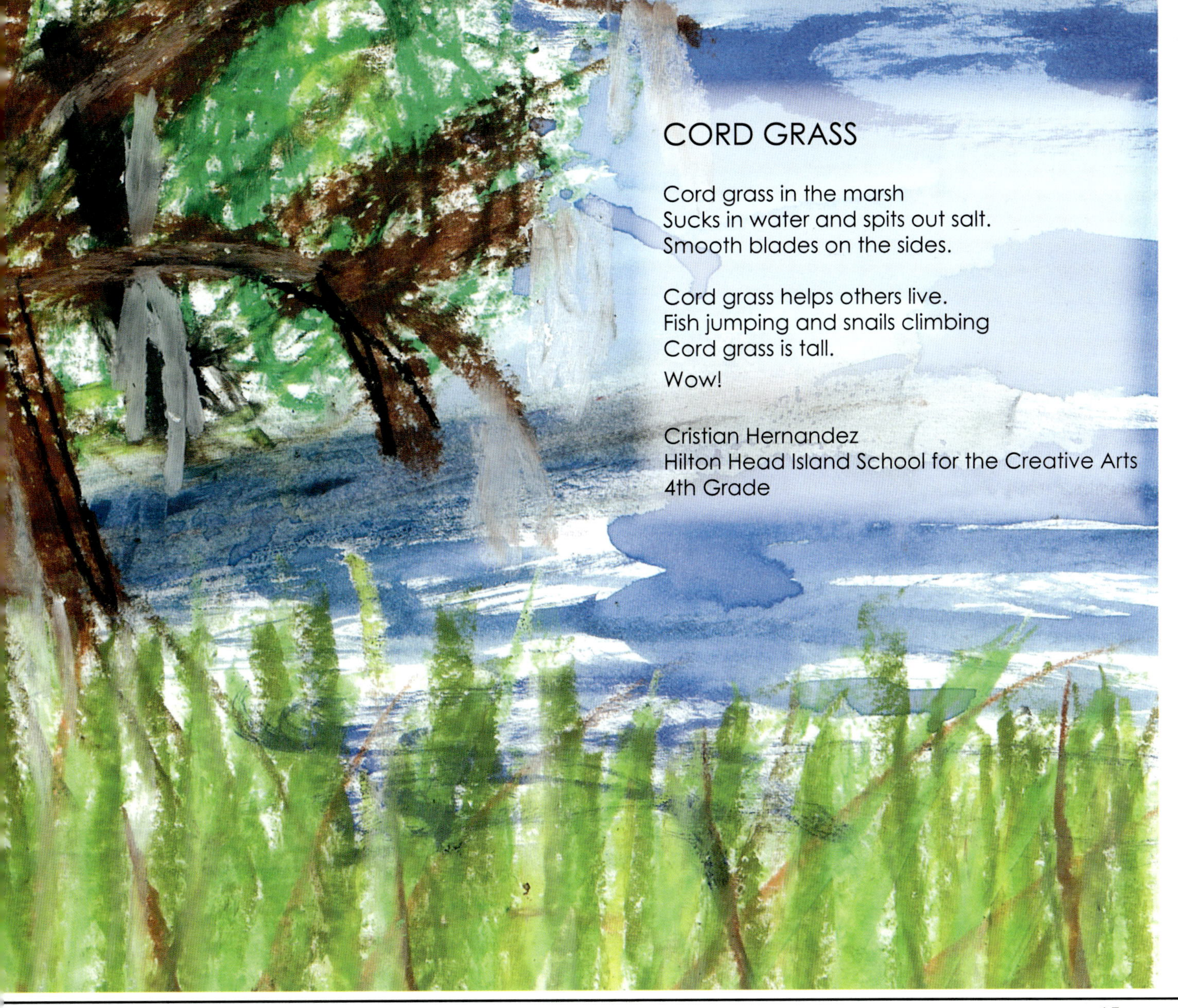

CORD GRASS

Cord grass in the marsh
Sucks in water and spits out salt.
Smooth blades on the sides.

Cord grass helps others live.
Fish jumping and snails climbing
Cord grass is tall.
Wow!

Cristian Hernandez
Hilton Head Island School for the Creative Arts
4th Grade

FIDDLER CRABS

I am a critter. I am a crawler.
My life is hard, much harder than yours.
I struggle to survive every second of the day. Predators everywhere I turn.

Raccoons, birds and snakes are only some I must deal with.
That's why I have 360 degree sight.
My back is turned when you try to sneak up on me, but I see you.

I move out of the way and run from you. I run into my tiny home.
It is one to two feet long, just big enough for me.
You try to find me, but you can't because I am brown and I camouflage into my surroundings.

You give up and go away. After you leave I come out of my hole.
I'm not scared,
I'm TERRIFIED!

Jamie Cosgrove
H.E. McCracken Middle
8th Grade

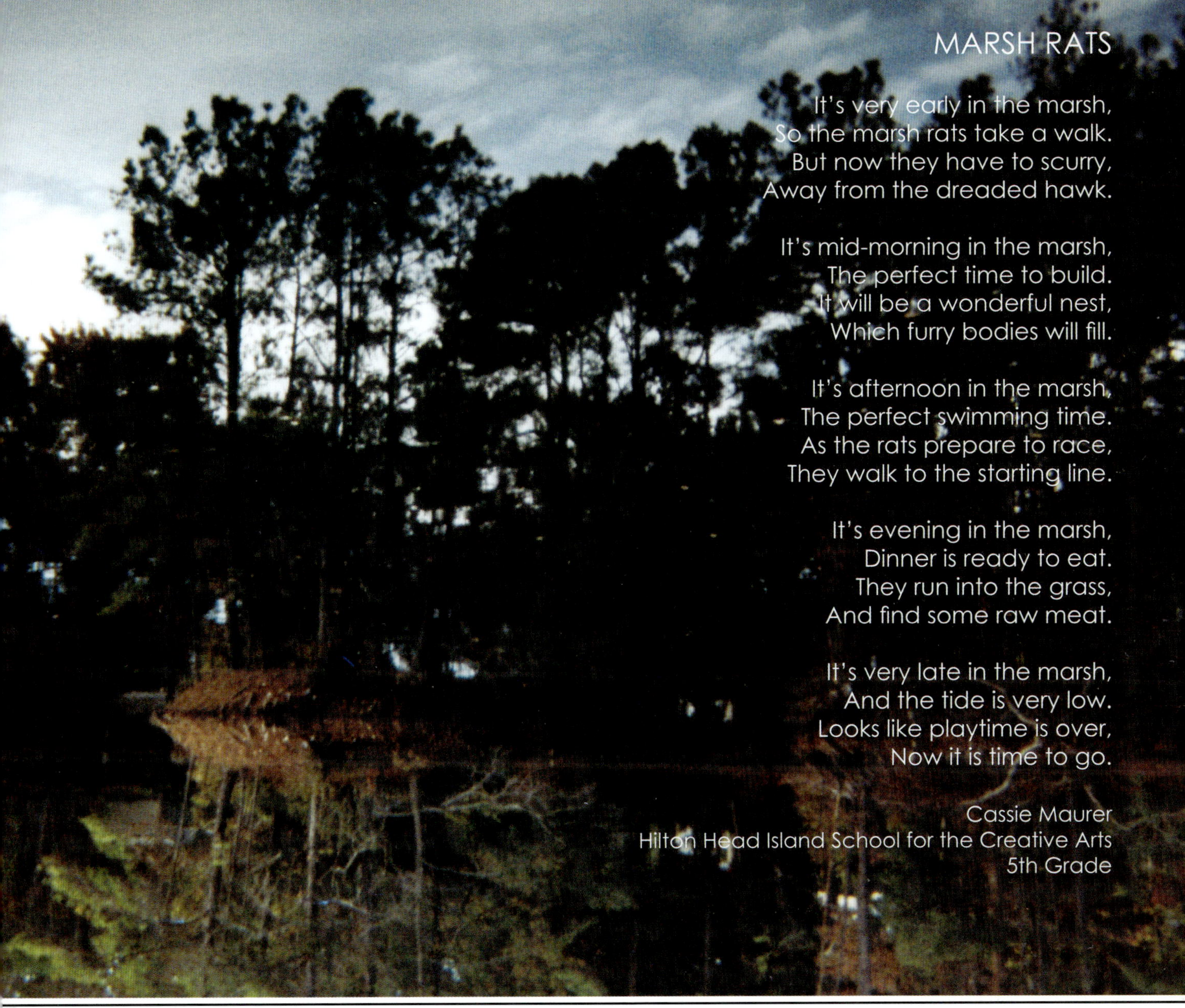

MARSH RATS

It's very early in the marsh,
So the marsh rats take a walk.
But now they have to scurry,
Away from the dreaded hawk.

It's mid-morning in the marsh,
The perfect time to build.
It will be a wonderful nest,
Which furry bodies will fill.

It's afternoon in the marsh,
The perfect swimming time.
As the rats prepare to race,
They walk to the starting line.

It's evening in the marsh,
Dinner is ready to eat.
They run into the grass,
And find some raw meat.

It's very late in the marsh,
And the tide is very low.
Looks like playtime is over,
Now it is time to go.

Cassie Maurer
Hilton Head Island School for the Creative Arts
5th Grade

FRANKLIN

Josh Brendler
Bluffton Middle School

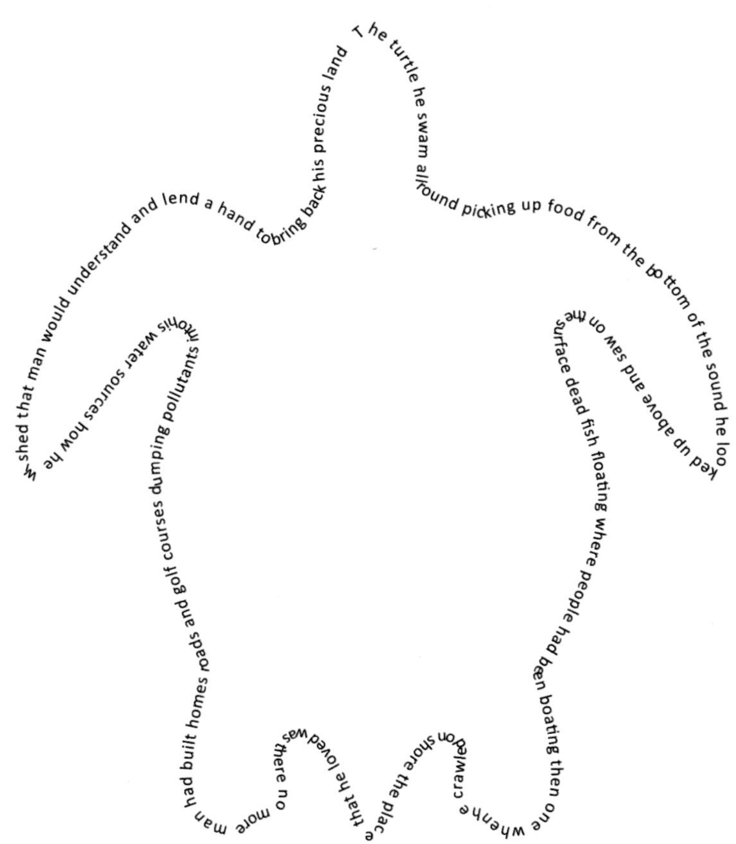

THE SUN

The sun rises and sets.
It leaves a shadow
on the waves of nature.
It's quiet except for
the sound of the waves
on the shore.
Will it ever stop
or has it even started?

Cloey Marcil
Robert Smalls Middle
7th Grade

MARSH LAND

Do you hear it?
The quiet sound of the spartina grass
blowing in the wind.
Do you feel it?
The gentle wind blowing on your face.
Do you smell it?
The saltiness of the beautiful
abundant ocean.

Cloey Marcil
Robert Smalls Middle
7th Grade

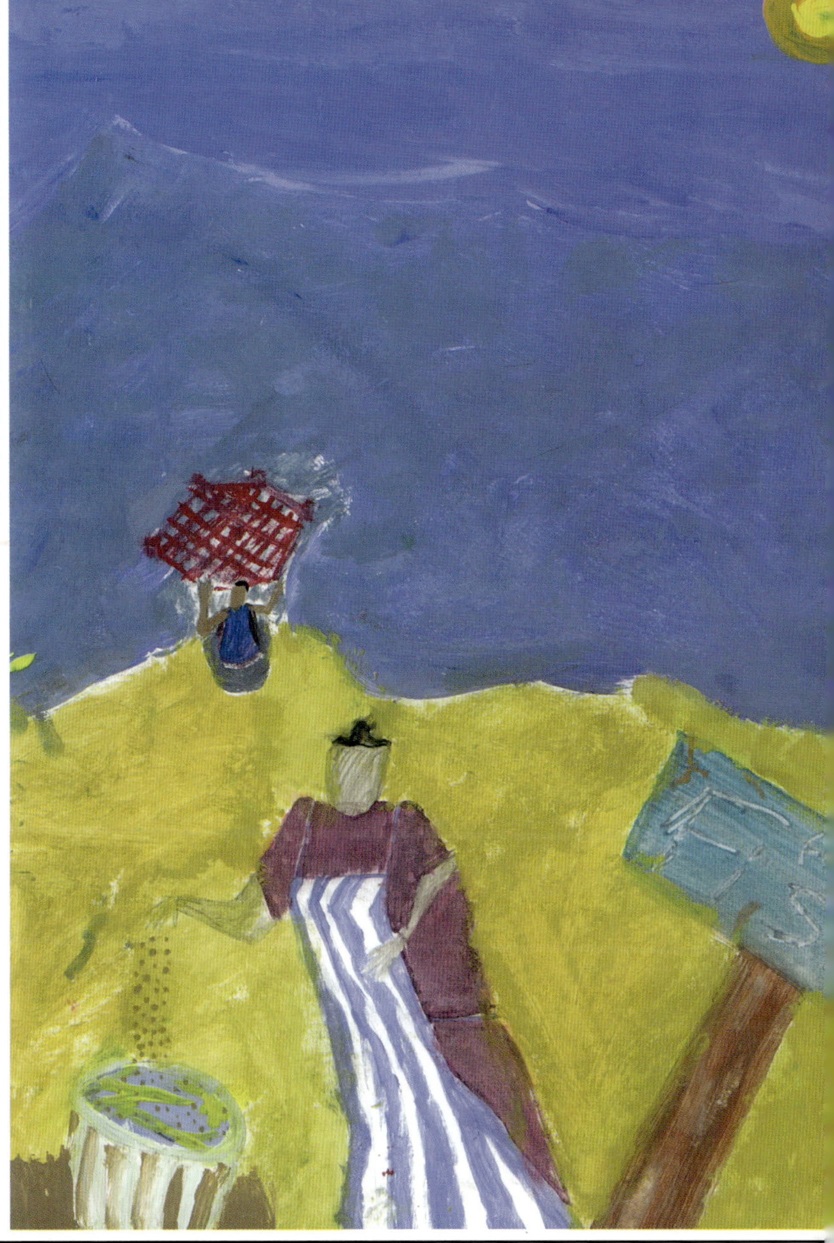

RIVER POEM

The movement of the water is so silent.
Waves sway back and forth to the nice beautiful sound.
Shrimps jump out of the water ready to be eaten.
Bottlenose dolphins hop out doing tricks.
Eastern Brown Pelicans fly down to swoop at their food.
River patrol boats make sure everyone is being correct.
People run toward the river trying to get oysters for dinner.
Sharks swim to catch their prey.
Crabs move quickly under the water.
Fish swim away so they don't get eaten.
Clams protect the little babies.
People have picnics and enjoy themselves on the banks.
Children play and have a good time.
Old people yell bingo, move checkers and click their teeth.
That's what happens at the river.

Tamia Rivers
Beaufort Elementary
5th Grade

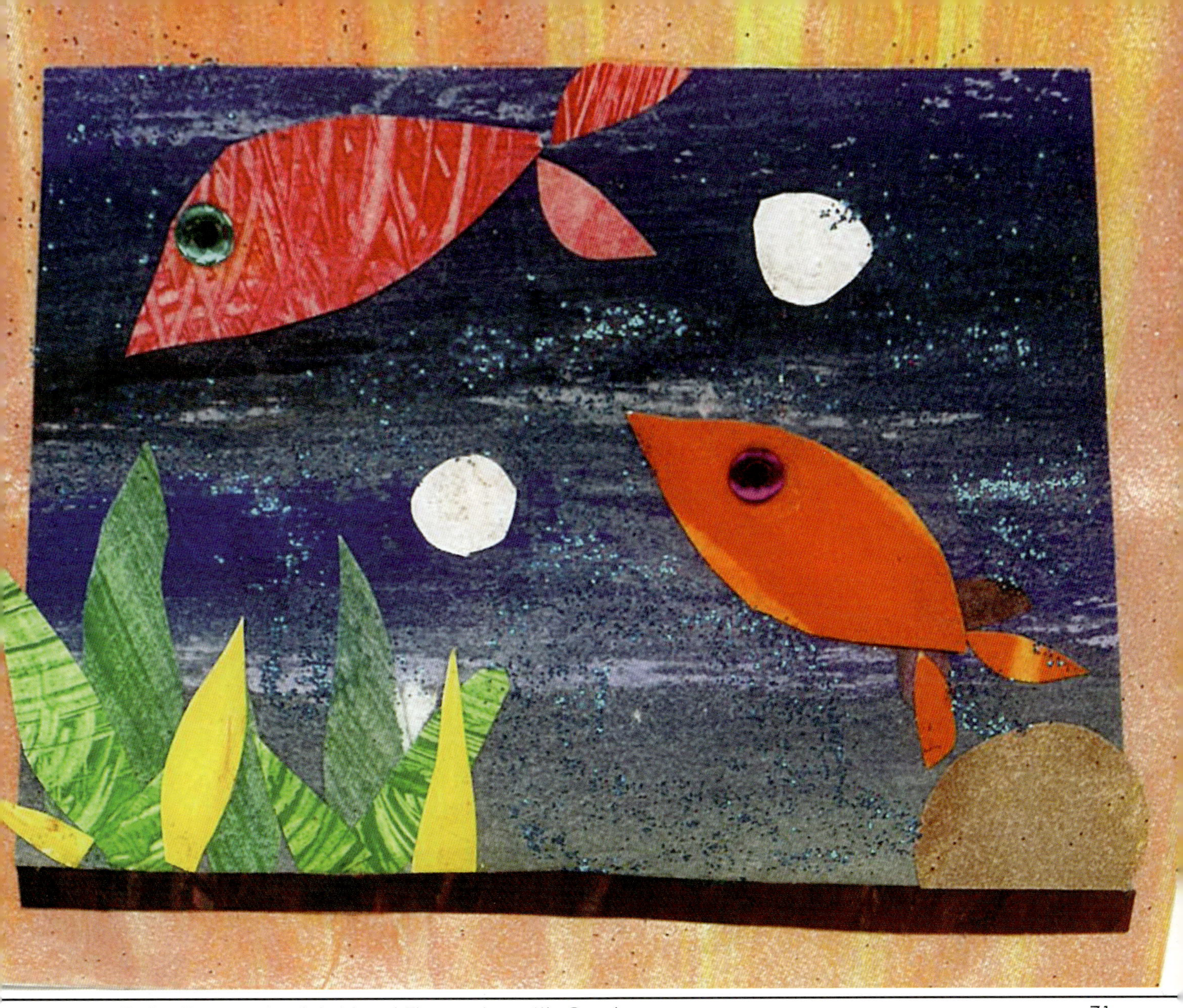

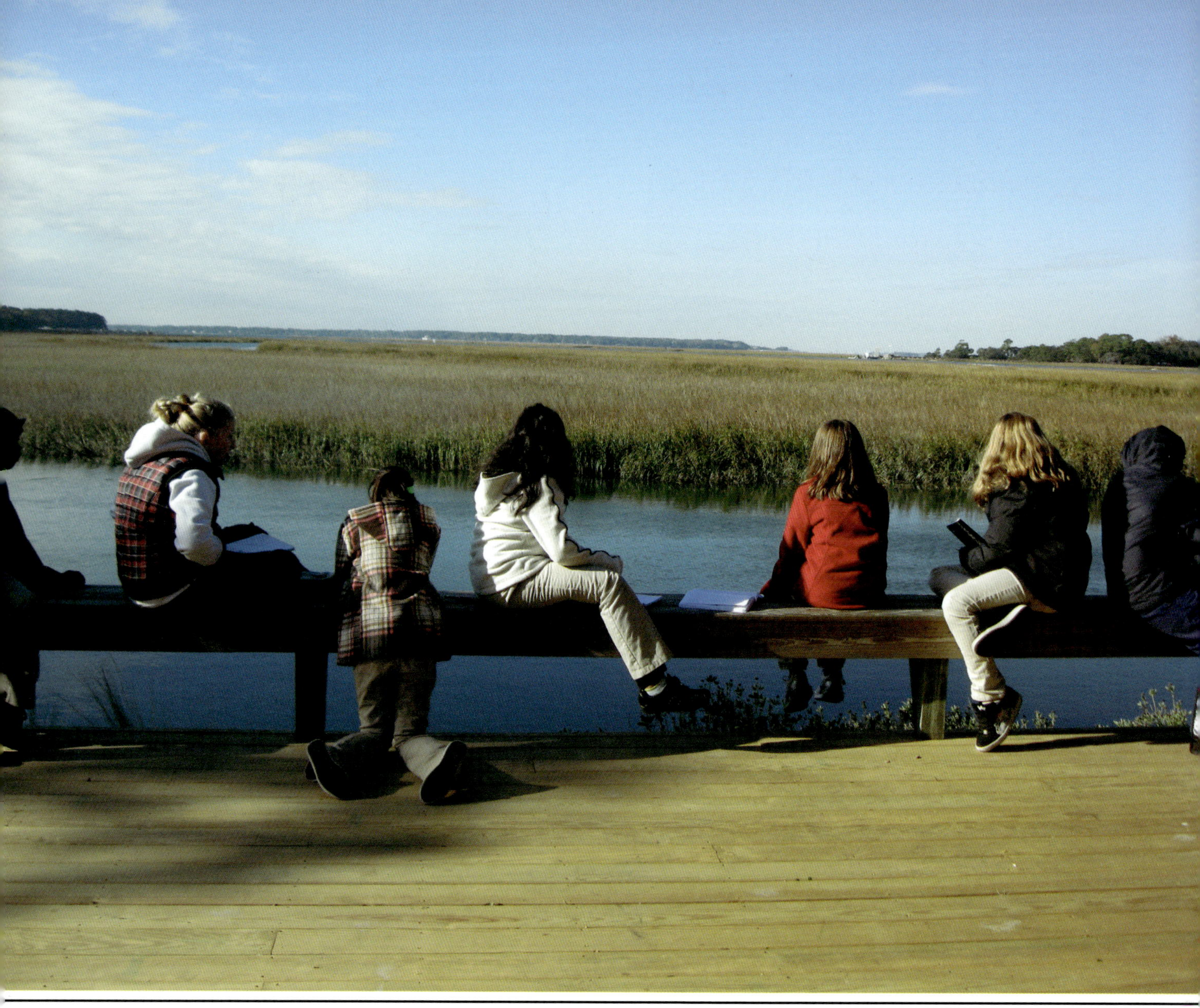

72

5th Grade Muses:Pritchardville Elementary

MYSTERIES UNDER THE OCEAN

Caught in the grasp of the ocean
Buried in the cold wet sand
Isolated and lonely
Waiting to be touched by a hand
White, brown, yellow and green
Petite or large, skinny or wide
Smooth, rough, bumpy or flat
Tumbling in with the tide
Used for throwing and tossing
Ornaments to hang on walls
Or decorate the ocean floor
And topping sand castles so tall
But the ones not seen by us
The ones underneath
Are waiting to be discovered
Are waiting to be seen
Caught in the grasp of the ocean
Buried in the cold wet sand
Mysteries under the ocean
Waiting to be touched by a hand.

Alexa Sebestyen
Beaufort Middle
8th Grade

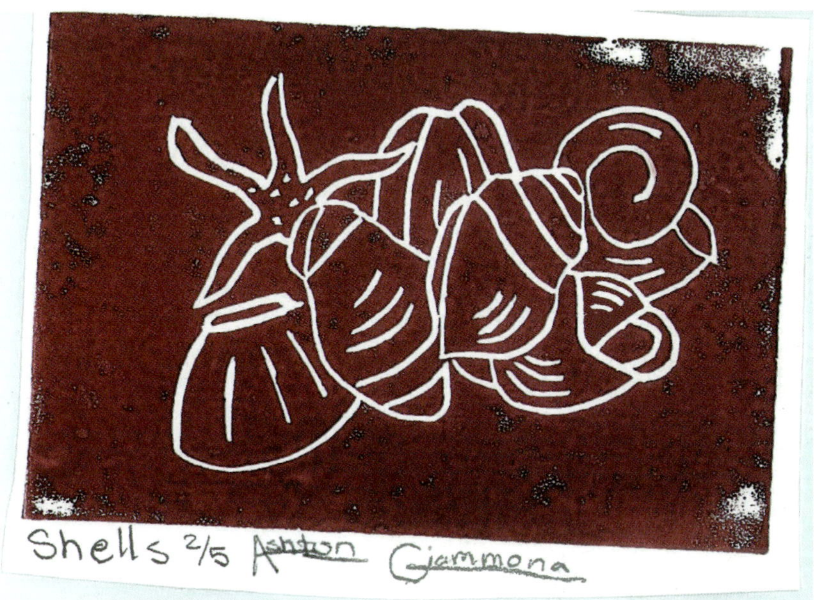

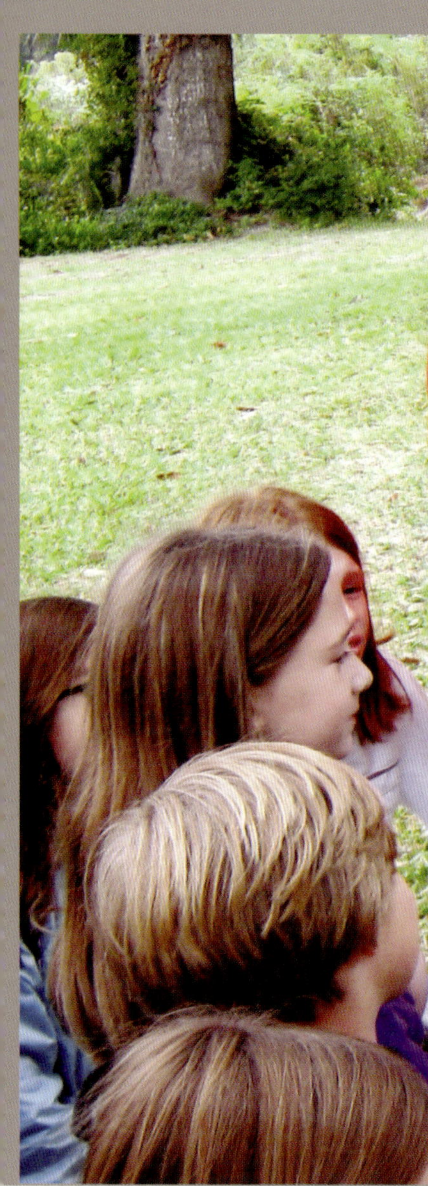

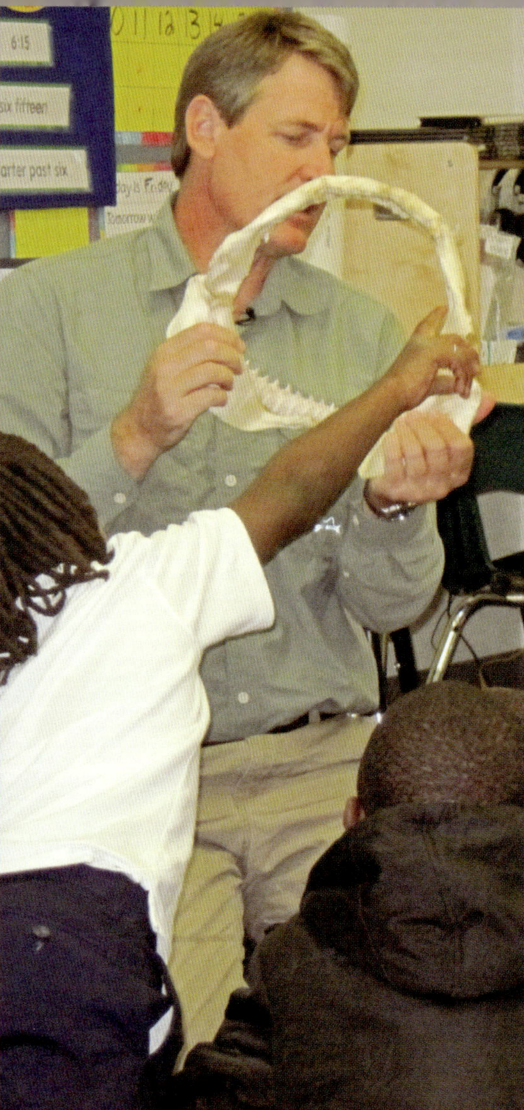

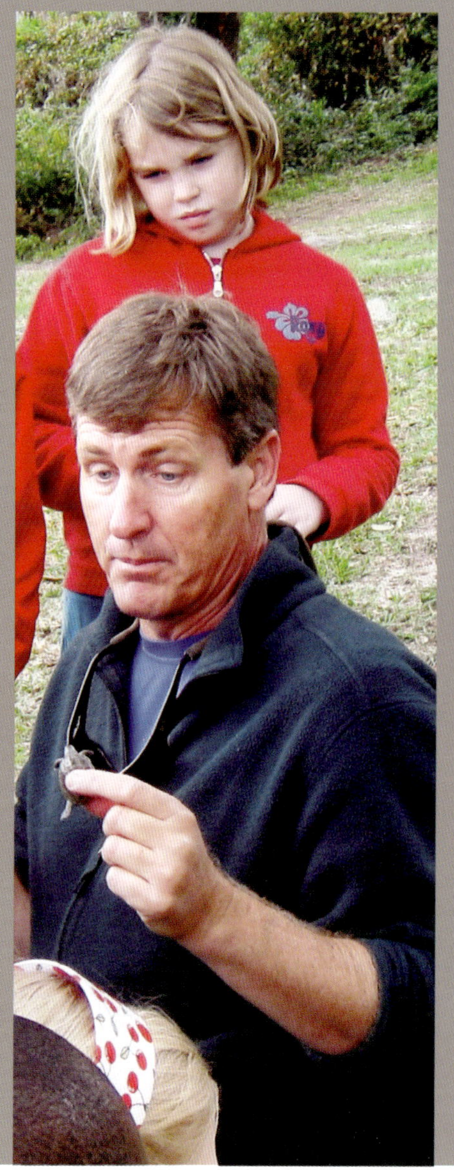

Naturalist Tony Mills LowCountry Institute

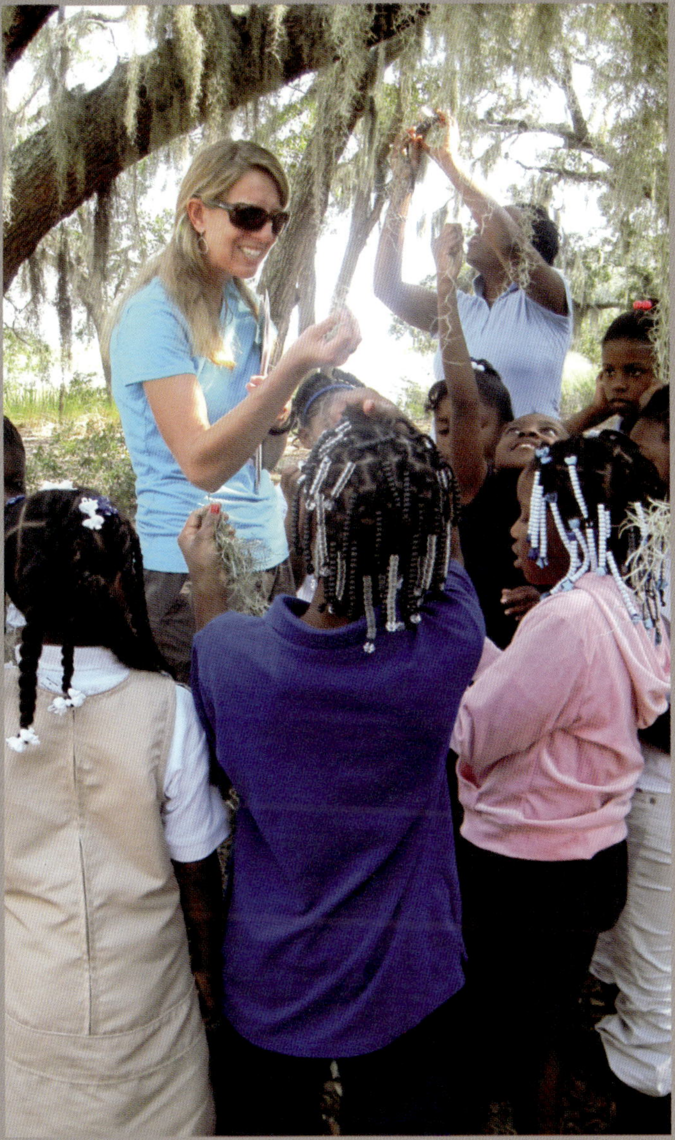

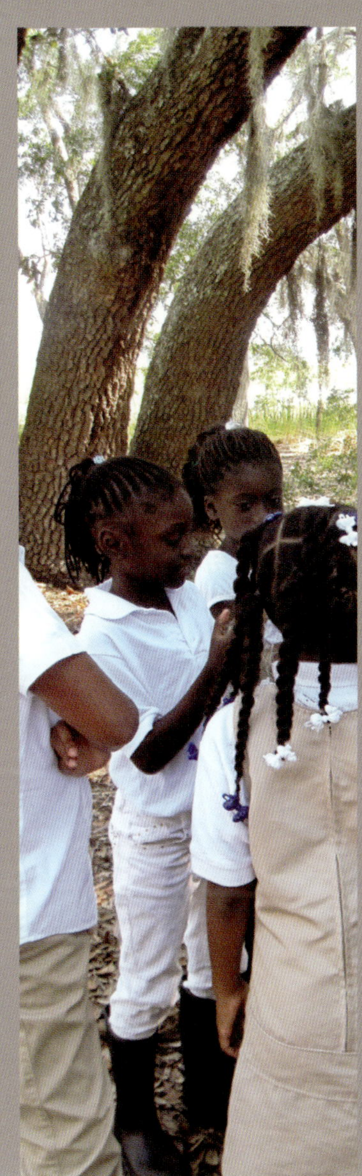
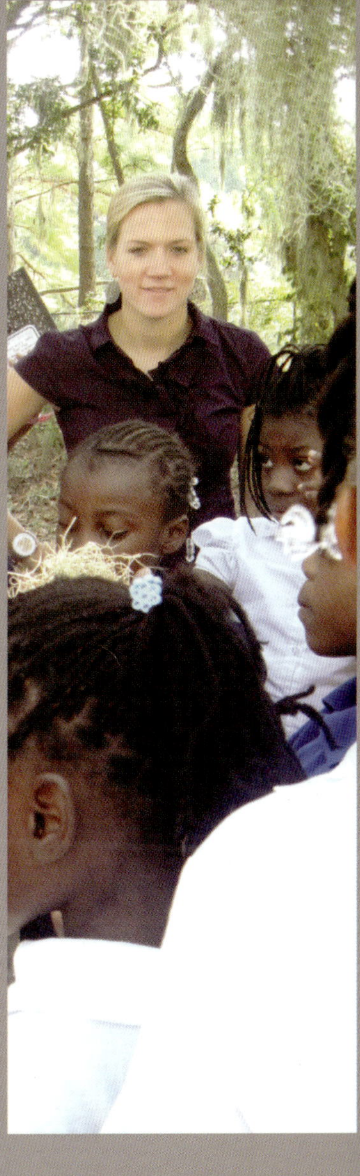

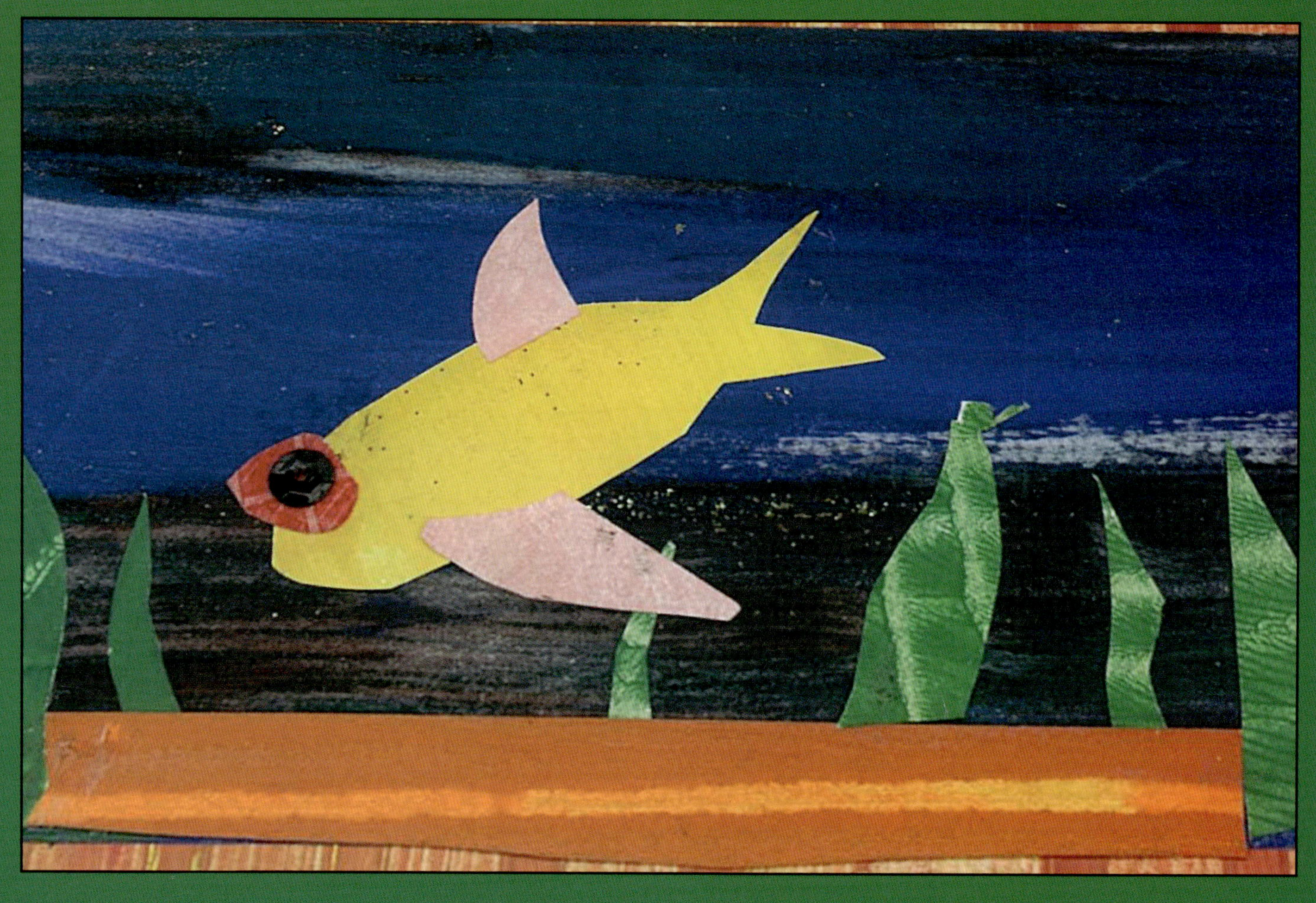

 Amelia Evans Lady's Island Elementary 4th Grade

A SILENT PREDATOR

Katie Hanley
Bluffton Middle School

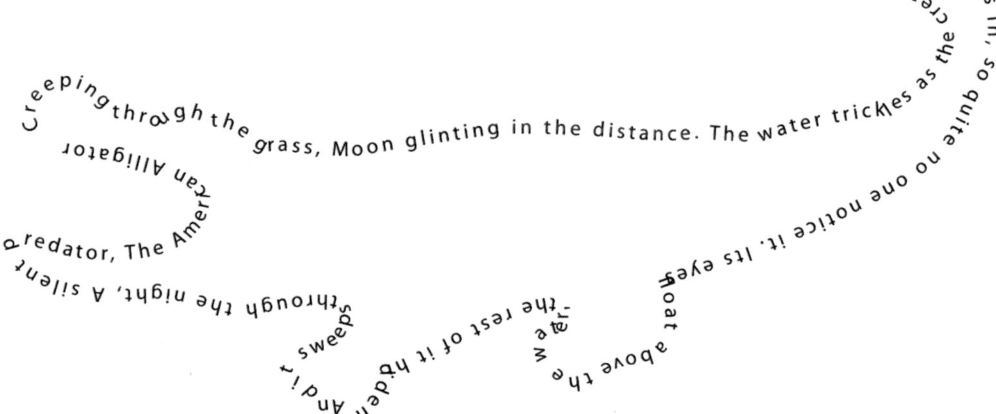

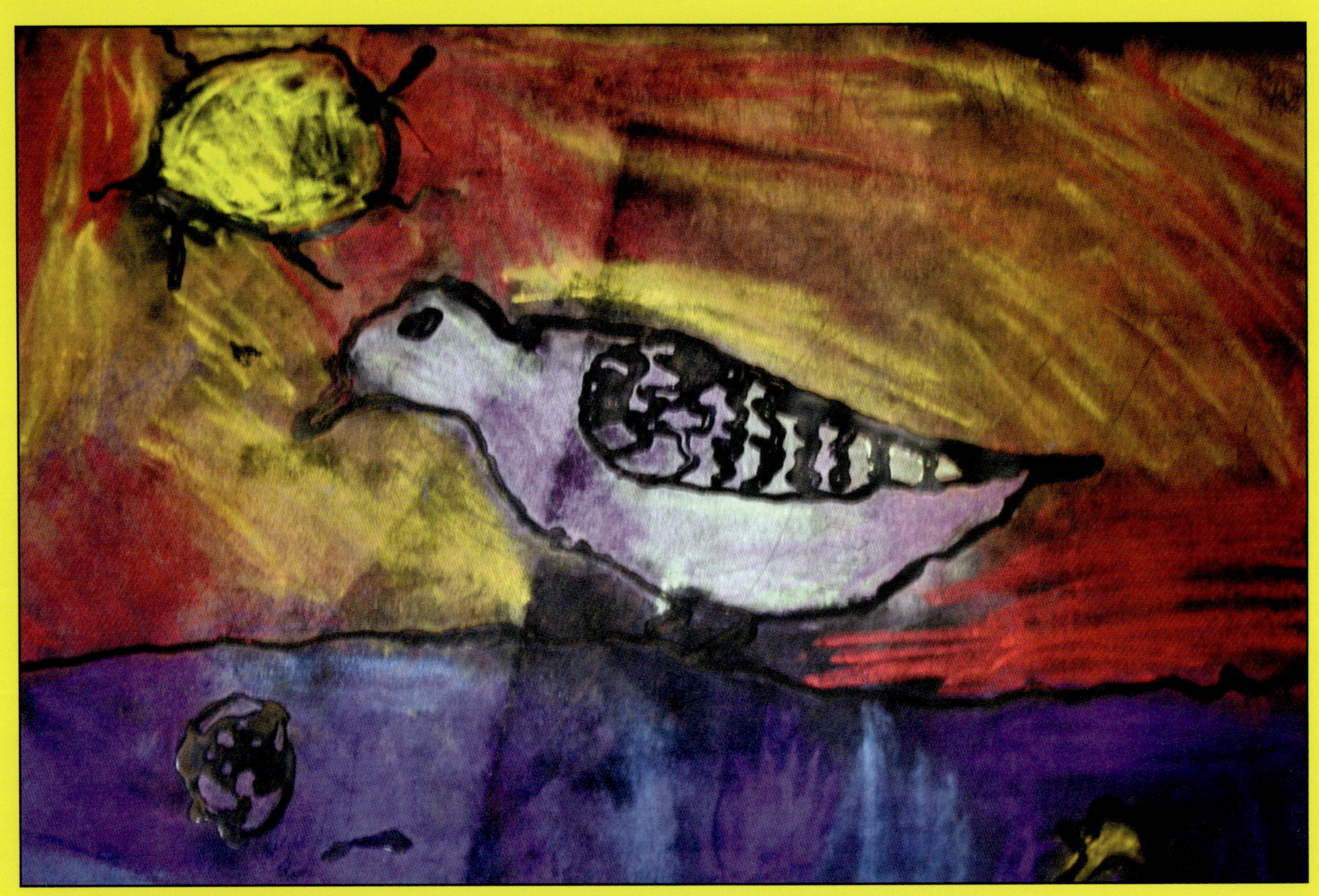

Alexandra Fisher Hilton Head Island School for the Creative Arts 1st Grade

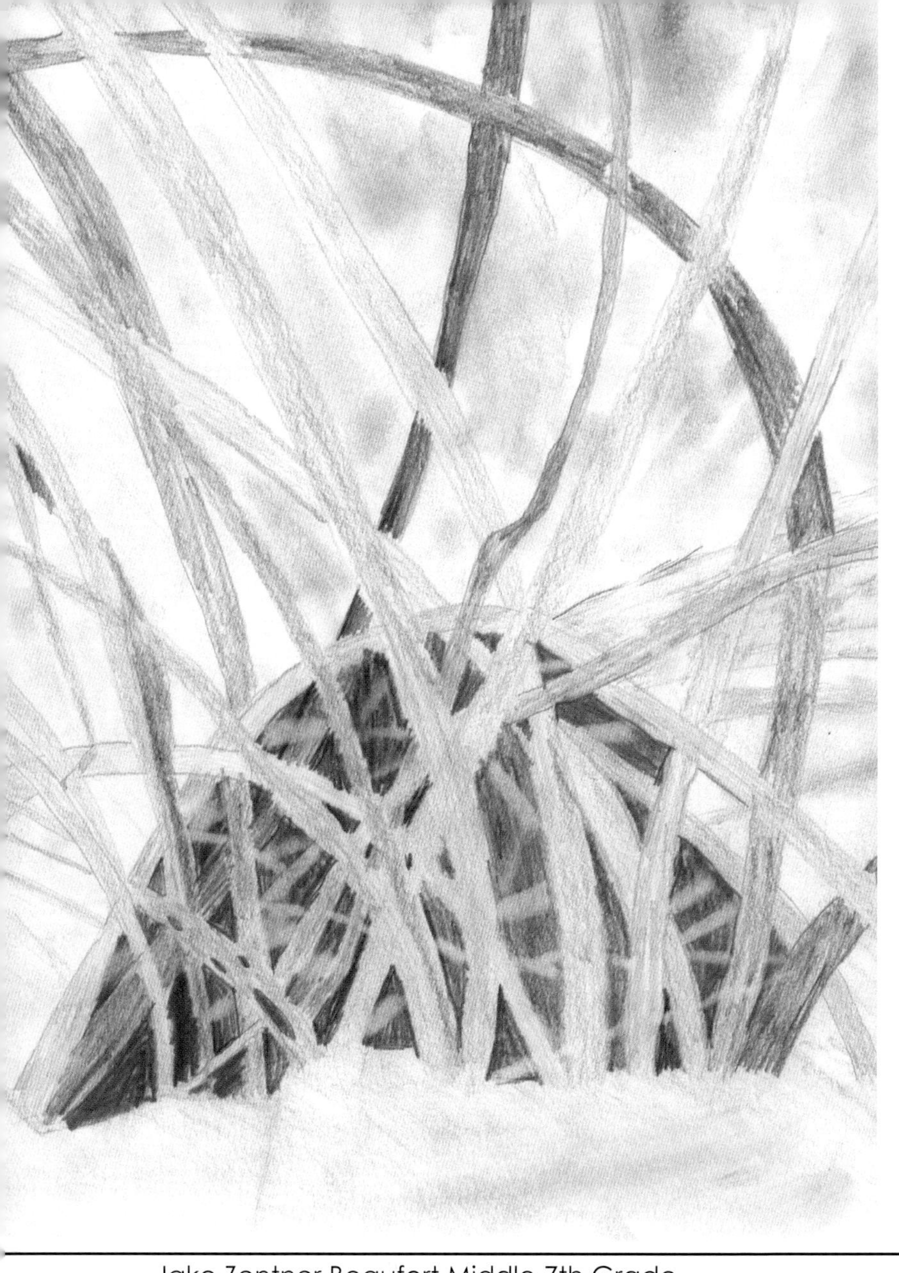

FALLING SLOWLY

The inferior plant is slanted slightly
On a never-ending beach with fine sand
In a constant battle with shimmering sea
In which none wins.

The plant feels trapped in the middle
Wishing to go to refuge with the forest
To be safe and happy
While it lasts.

The plant is sad, he knows his fate
One day he will be swallowed
By shimmering aqua perfection.

Jake Zentner
Beaufort Middle
7th Grade

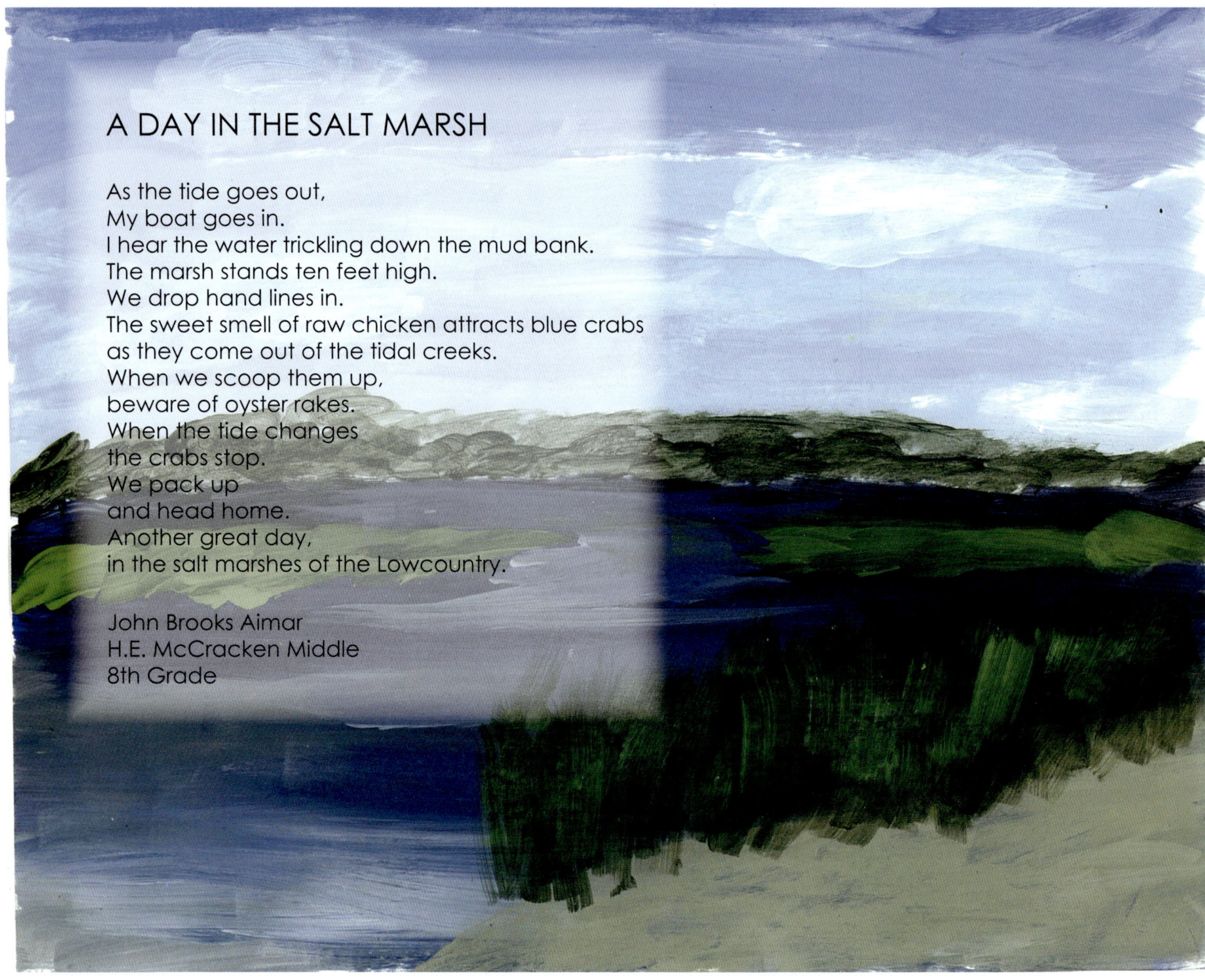

A DAY IN THE SALT MARSH

As the tide goes out,
My boat goes in.
I hear the water trickling down the mud bank.
The marsh stands ten feet high.
We drop hand lines in.
The sweet smell of raw chicken attracts blue crabs
as they come out of the tidal creeks.
When we scoop them up,
beware of oyster rakes.
When the tide changes
the crabs stop.
We pack up
and head home.
Another great day,
in the salt marshes of the Lowcountry.

John Brooks Aimar
H.E. McCracken Middle
8th Grade

LIVE OAK

Anna Caroline Cribb
Bluffton Middle School

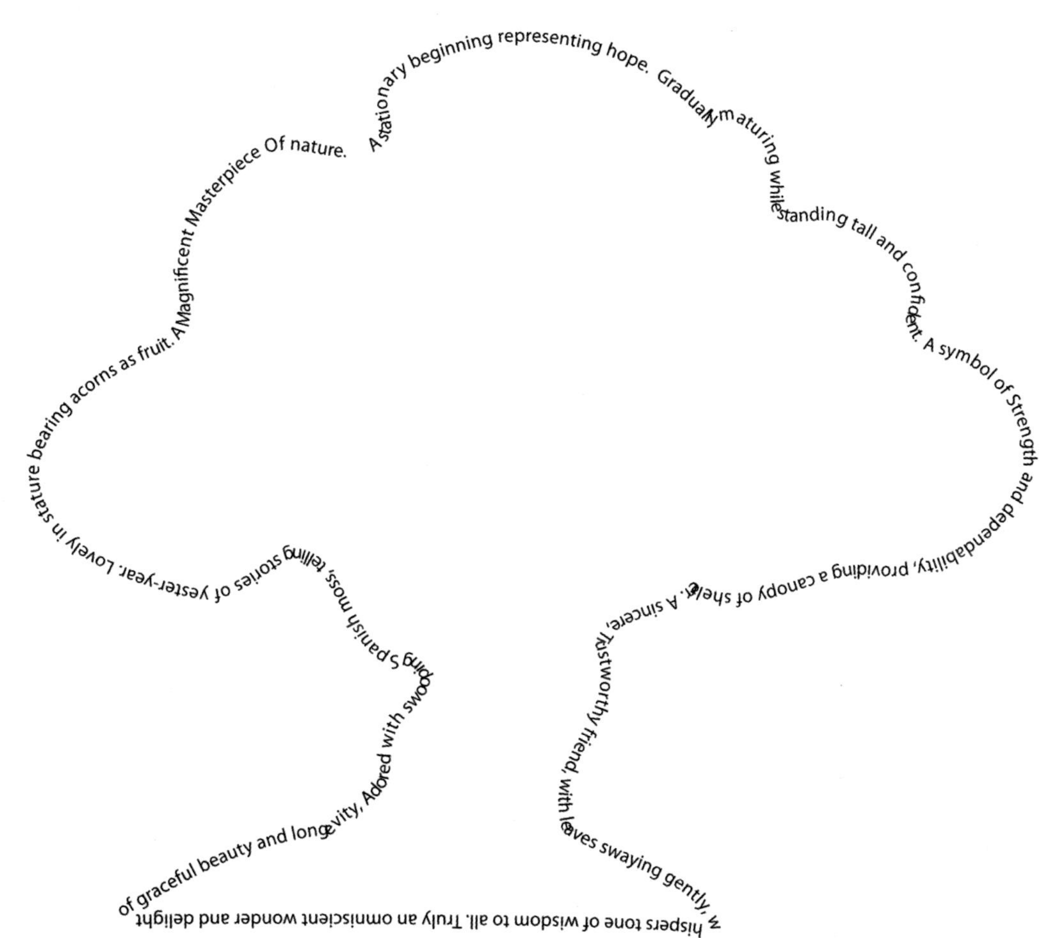

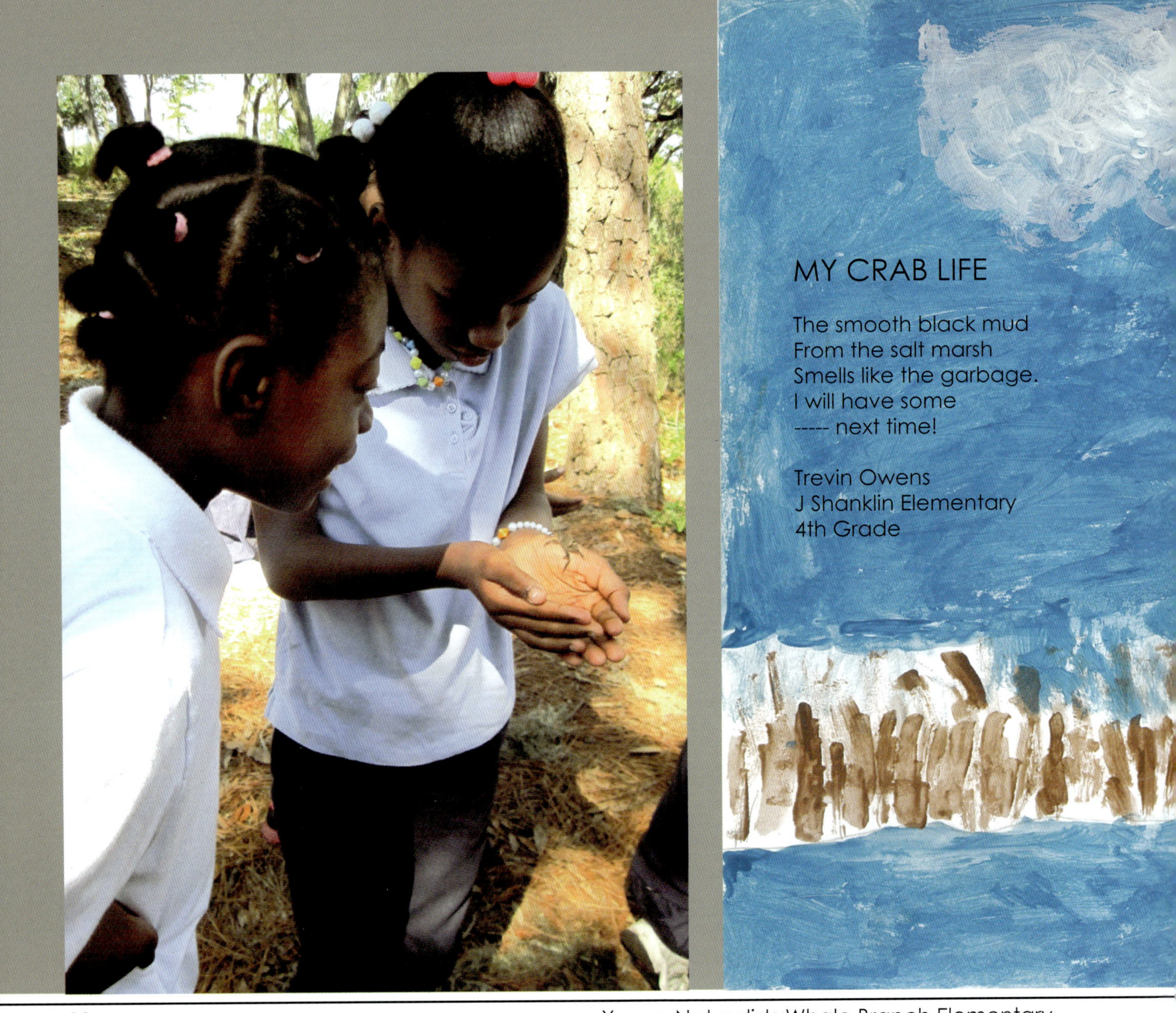

MY CRAB LIFE

The smooth black mud
From the salt marsh
Smells like the garbage.
I will have some
----- next time!

Trevin Owens
J Shanklin Elementary
4th Grade

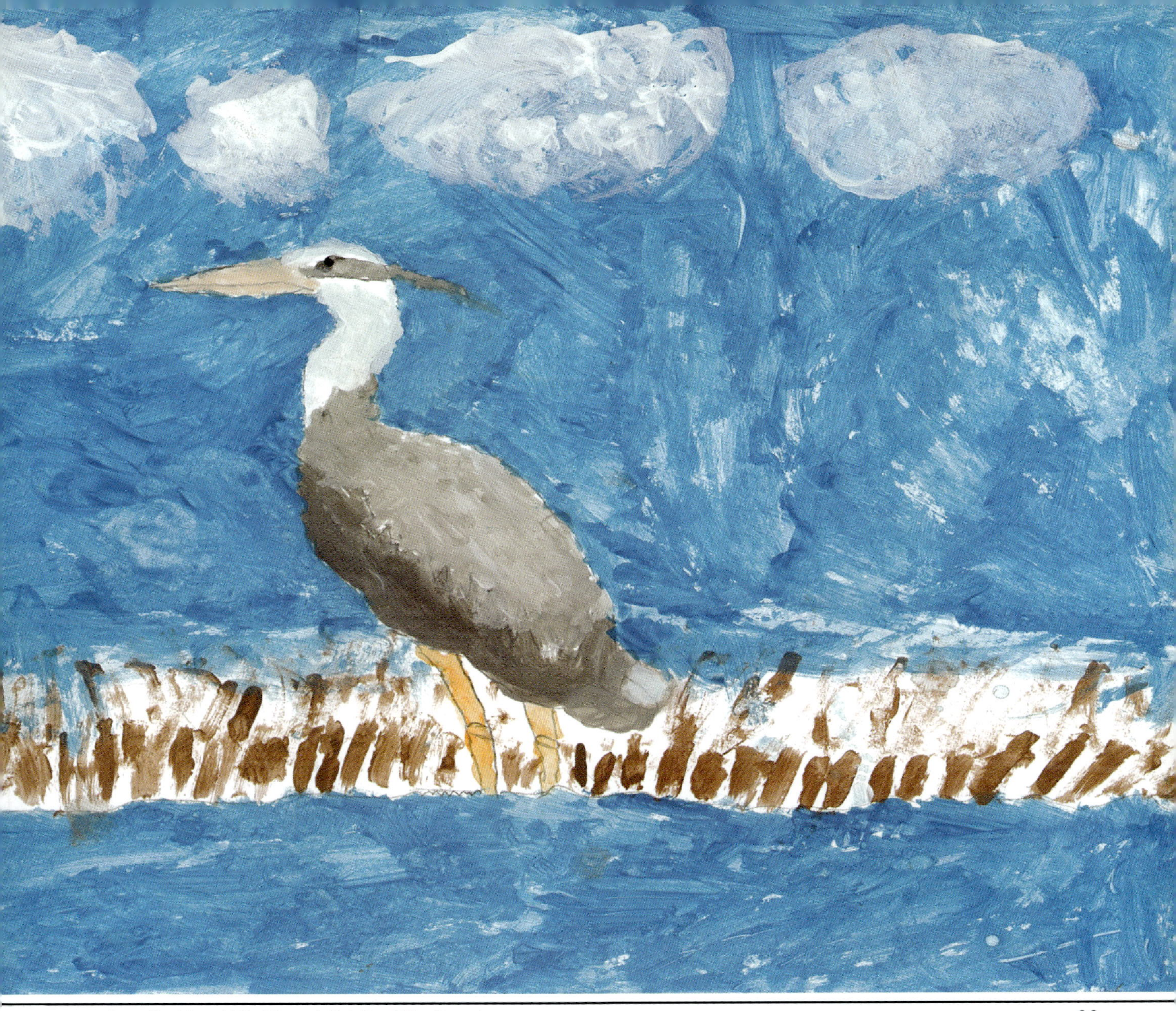

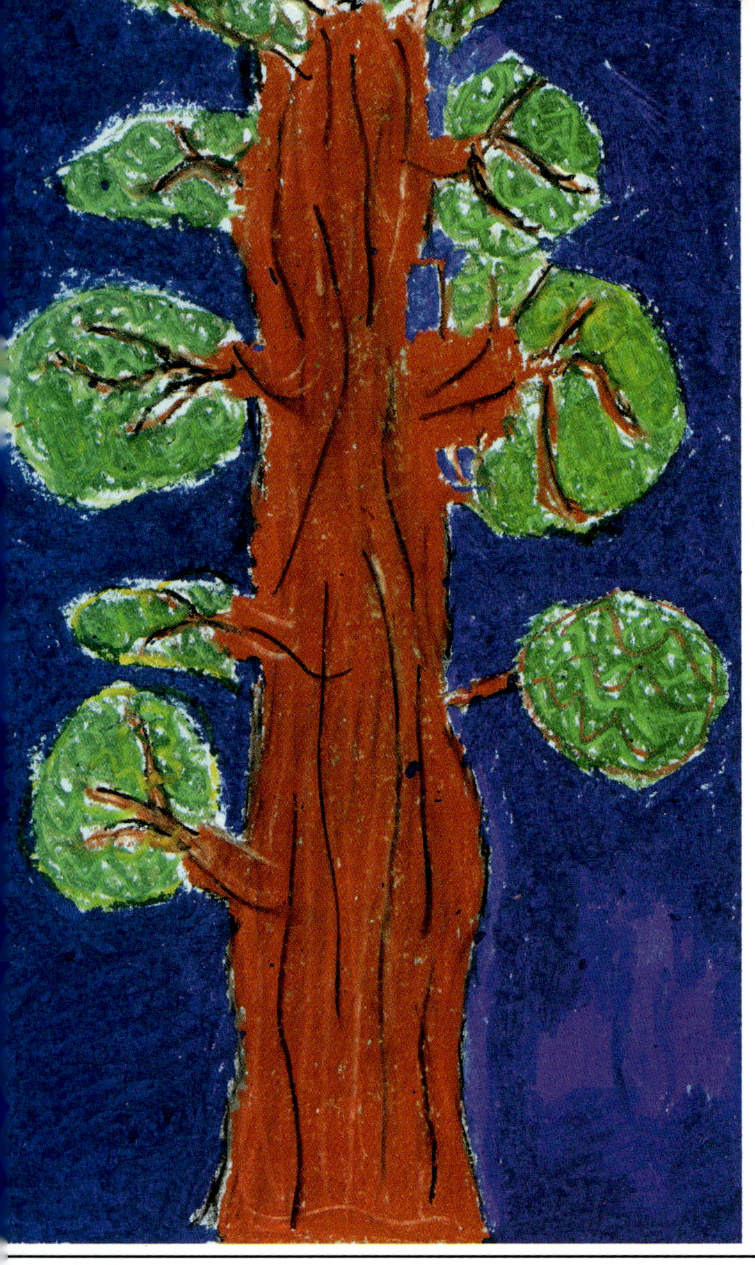

MANY THINGS

I have seen many things
I have witnessed it all
Some good, some not so much
I have seen it come and I have seen it go
I have seen it sparkle and glow
I have seen it neglected and trashed
I was a bystander watching helplessly
As they dumped in more and more
It couldn't take it anymore
It couldn't clean itself fast enough
So I started to die
I have lived by the beautiful May River
As long as I've been alive
I am a Water Oak
I have seen many things

Jaala Hutchinson
Bluffton Middle
7th Grade

Iliana Hebda Pritchardville Elementary 5th Grade

WINTER WILDLIFE

Moss sways in the gentle breeze
Flags in the distance fluttering in its force.
The icy wind whipping my face
Cold weather surrounds.

Loon swims by, making a commotion,
While fishing for next catch.
He dives under to snatch his meal
And surfaces with grace.
It is lunchtime.

Warning!
Alligators loom near.
Stay safe. Don't swim.
You might become their next meal.

Prowling cat, circling our bus,
Trying to catch a bird, preparing to
pounce.
The bird flies away to safety.
No lunch for Cat today.

Stone crabs, striped bass trapped in jail
As the bass gasps for air.
Crabs reach for it,
Wanting a meal.

Winter surrounds the earth.
Few animals show themselves,
Only the loon shows off.
Birds and cats play tag
While stone crabs and striped bass
remain in jail.

Winter is here to stay.

Audrey Palau
Pritchardville Elementary
5th Grade

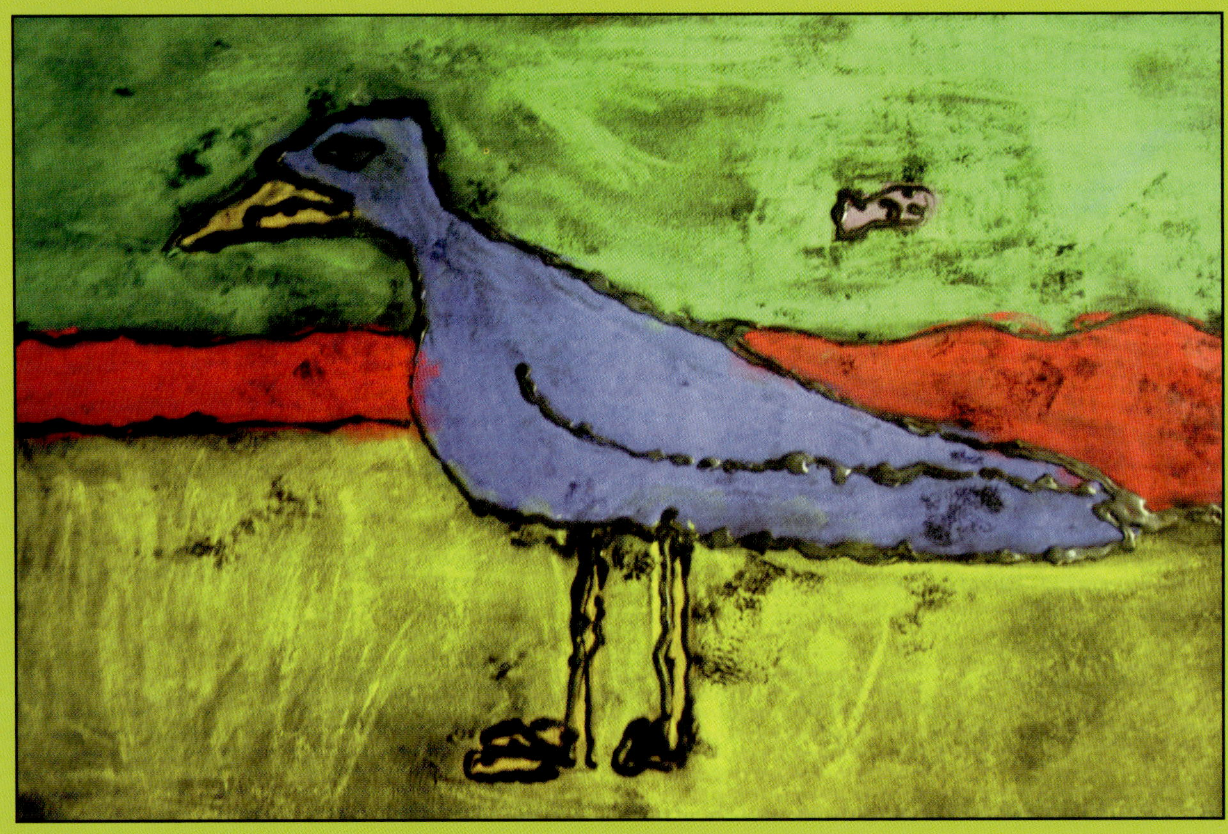

 Ana Fierros Hilton Head Island School for the Creative Arts 1st Grade

First and foremost, sincerest thanks to Master Naturalists who taught teachers and motivated students to inspect – and respect -- the uniqueness of the Port Royal Sound ecosystem: LowCountry Institute, Coastal Discovery Museum, Hunting Island State Park, Clemson Extension, Waddell Mariculture Center, Beaufort Conservation District, SC Department of Natural Resources, Outside Hilton Head, Waterdog Outfitters, A&B Charter Tours and Beaufort Kayak Tours.

Gratitude goes to the many creative geniuses who helped students merge science and art into imaginative products: Children's Author Kevin Kurtz, Poet Heather Magruder along with Visual Artists Mary Segars, Mandy Johnson, Melba Cooper, Kim Keats, Alana Adams, Mary Pratt, Brucie Holler, Russ Petty, Jim Schultz and Joe Rock Edwards. And to Liz Chase who magically transformed folders and folders of text and images into this extraordinary publication.

Tremendous kudos to the 130 teachers who accepted the challenge of adding "one more thing" to their instruction without really knowing what the expectations and outcomes would be. Cheers to participating schools: Beaufort Elementary, Broad River Elementary, Hilton Head Island Elementary, Hilton Head Island School for Creative Arts, Joseph Shanklin Elementary, Lady's Island Elementary, Pritchardville Elementary, Shell Point Elementary, Whale Branch Elementary, Beaufort Middle, Bluffton Middle, HE McCracken Middle, Lady's Island Middle, Robert Smalls Middle and Beaufort High.

Above all, standing ovations to the 2400 youth who listened and looked and learned to appreciate the majesty of Port Royal Sound. Their creative interpretations of the natural world never cease to amaze! These young environmentalists will be the voices of tomorrow, the stewards who carry on the work of protecting Beaufort County's pristine landscape.

None of this would be possible without the inspiration of the national River of Words program, and the generous financial and in-kind support of the Beaufort County Board of Education and community partners Port Royal Sound Fund, Arts Council of Beaufort County and Arts Center of Coastal Carolina. Special thanks to very special donors Sharon and Dick Stewart. With final tribute going to Superintendent Valerie Truesdale, whose keen vision and strong leadership steer the course in making good things happen for children.

Deepest appreciation to you all!
Margaret Rushton, Project Director and Fine Arts Coordinator
Sherry Carroll, English Language Arts Coordinator
Karenanne Koenig, Science Coordinator
Dr. Anne Pressley, Director of Teaching and Learning
Dr. Sean Alford, Chief Instructional Officer
Beaufort County School District, Beaufort, South Carolina

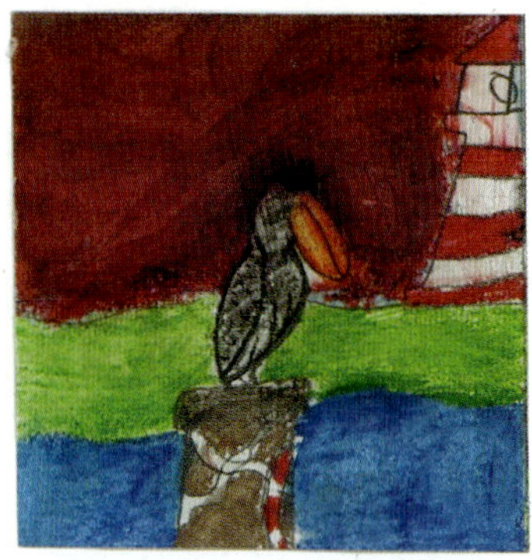

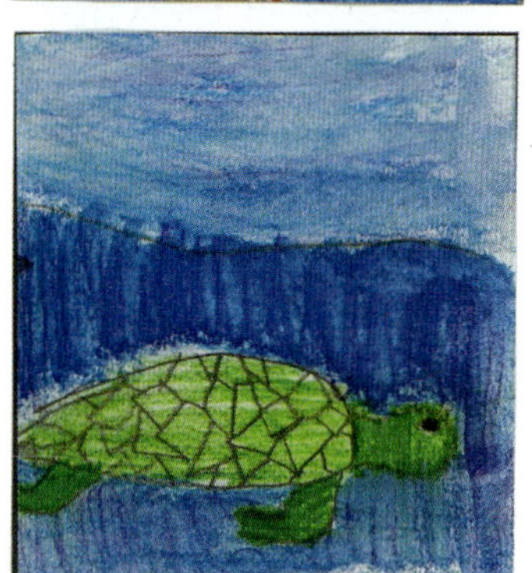

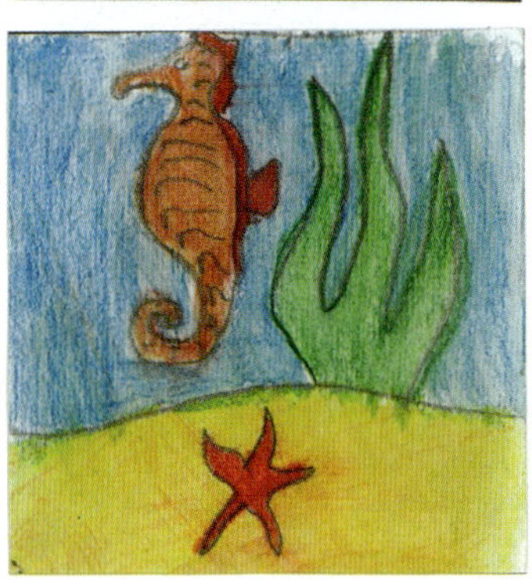

Port Royal Sound

Beaufort County's Port Royal Sound is a marriage of ocean and land, a relationship created by the combination of rising sea level, exceptionally high tides, and its unique geology. The synergistic combination of these three factors has produced a marine environment that is one of North America's overlooked ecological jewels.

Three factors make Port Royal Sound different from other coastal areas. First, the area receives its freshwater primarily through runoff rather than from rivers. Despite the "river" in their names, the Broad, Colleton, and May Rivers are actually salt water "fingers" extending inland because most of their flow comes from the ocean in the form of tides, rather than from the uplands in the form of runoff.

Secondly, the rising sea level has slowly flooded the original coastal landscape, turning former valleys into deep tidal creeks and hilltops into islands surrounded by salt marsh. Local tidal creeks and waterways are deep because of the absence of freshwater rivers emptying sediment into this system. As a result, half of Beaufort County is covered by marine waters.

The third major factor is the exceptional high tides found in this area. The tidal amplitude (difference between high and low tide) ranges from 6 feet during neap tides to over 10 feet during Spring tides. The lack of freshwater and the large areas of submerged coastal terrain in Beaufort County combine to create expansive marshes of Spartina alterniflora, the only species of plant that grows in salt water in temperate North America. Consequently, Beaufort County has the distinction of having at least 50% of South Carolina's salt marsh.